- WHEN, WHERE, AND HOW DO YOU TAKE BEST ADVANTAGE OF DISCOUNTS?

- WHAT IS INVOLVED IN THE LEGAL-FINANCIAL ASPECTS OF A PARTNERSHIP?

- HOW ARE PAYROLL TAXES COMPUTED—WHERE ARE THERE SAVINGS FOR THE EMPLOYER?

- CAN A BUSINESS BUY ON CREDIT AND STILL BE WORTH WHAT THE BALANCE SHEET INDICATES?

The answer to all these questions, and many more may be found on the pages of this book. Here is an important guide to the fundamentals of accounting by a leading expert, who explains how to get the most out of money, from corporate finance to sugar-bowl change.

An investment in **AN ACCOUNTING PRIMER** *is an investment in your future.*

Titles of Special Interest
from the MENTOR Executive Library

AN
ACCOUNTING
PRIMER

by Elwin W. Midgett

Professor, Department of Business Education
Middle Tennessee State University, Murfreesboro

A MENTOR BOOK
NEW AMERICAN LIBRARY
TIMES MIRROR
NEW YORK AND SCARBOROUGH, ONTARIO
THE NEW ENGLISH LIBRARY LIMITED, LONDON

Library of Congress Catalog Card Number: 68-54321

 MENTOR TRADEMARK REG. U.S. PAT. OFF. AND FOREIGN COUNTRIES
REGISTERED TRADEMARK—MARCA REGISTRADA
HECHO EN CHICAGO, U.S.A.

SIGNET, SIGNET CLASSICS, MENTOR, PLUME AND MERIDIAN BOOKS
are published *in the United States* by
The New American Library, Inc.,
1301 Avenue of the Americas, New York, New York, 10019,
in Canada by The New American Library of Canada Limited,
81 Mack Avenue, Scarborough, 704, Ontario,
in the United Kingdom by The New English Library Limited,
Barnard's Inn, Holborn, London, E.C. 1, England.

FIRST MENTOR PRINTING, OCTOBER, 1968

5 6 7 8 9 10 11 12 13

PRINTED IN THE UNITED STATES OF AMERICA

To Nell

Contents

Preface

Accounting has been called the "heart" of business and few people would disagree with this statement. More and more it is becoming imperative that young executives, management trainees and all businessmen become knowledgeable in this subject.

At any meeting of a group of businessmen, whether a civic club, country club or church board, the author is always amazed at the total lack of understanding of a balance sheet or a profit and loss statement. Although the author does not believe that this situation is one that calls for immediate action, he has attempted to include in this book some ideas, gleaned from twenty-five years of classroom instruction in accounting, that may be of help to anyone who needs, or would like to have, a knowledge of this subject, regardless of his profession. The author has included many shortcuts, learned from experience, that may be of help to bookkeepers who are already on the job.

The purpose of this book is simply to make accounting principles easy to understand. Because this book is written in clear, concise terms, it will enable a busy person to save time, and can make a valuable contribution to his general education without forcing him to read a difficult eight or nine-hundred-page textbook.

The author wishes to thank Professor Henrietta Wade of Middle Tennessee State University for her invaluable aid in the production of the book, and particularly for her encouragement during the book's formative stages.

Chapter 1

GETTING THE RIGHT START

ACCOUNTING PRINCIPLES have not changed since an Italian monk, Fra Luca Pacioli, introduced the double entry system in 1494. This fact should encourage anyone who is beginning the study of accounting. Here is a subject that can be learned, the principles of which will not change as long as $1 + 1 = 2$, or better still, as long as $2 = 1 + 1$.

Accounting will be easy to learn if the fundamental accounting equation, Assets = Liabilities + Proprietorship, is understood thoroughly. The importance of a complete understanding of this equation cannot be overemphasized. The balance sheet, the most important business statement, is based upon the equation. The theory of debit and credit or the "how" of recording business transactions becomes simple and certain with the proper understanding of this equation. No one ever gets away from the influence of this equation in his study of accounting. In learning problems of an advanced nature, such as the preparation of a work sheet for a "Statement of Application of Funds," he will find this equation a most valuable tool.

To understand the equation one must understand the words used in it. Assets are things of value that someone owns—the watch on his wrist, the money in his pocket or in the bank, the clothes on his back, the automobile he drives. Some of these may not be completely paid for, but if they are in his possession, and he has title to them,

11

they are his assets. A business has assets also. Its merchandise, furniture, fixtures and building are examples. The business may not have paid in full for all its assets, but someone owns them.

Liabilities means debts. Accounts that are owed, notes that are owed, anything that is owed, such as rent, wages and utilities, are liabilities.

Proprietorship, net worth, or capital is the difference between what a person or a business owns (assets) and what is owed (liabilities). Naturally, if a business had $10 in assets and owed $5, it would be worth $5.

A going or solvent business is pictured in this manner:

The seesaw is balanced and it will always be as long as the business stays solvent. An individual or a business can go into debt to the extent that liabilities are greater than assets. When that occurs, the seesaw comes tumbling down.

To learn accounting, one must print this equation indelibly on his mind: $A = L + P \ldots A = L + P \ldots A = L + P$. This is the foundation on which a knowledge of accounting is built. One should have a thorough understanding of the equation. If he does not, he must have faith that "A" does equal "L" plus "P."

Also, seen as:

Assets = Equity

Chapter II

THE BALANCE SHEET

THE PURPOSE of the balance sheet is to show the financial condition of a business at any given date. The balance sheet is the most important statement that an accountant prepares. It says to anyone reading it, "Here is the result of all the transactions that this business has ever had from its very first transaction years and years ago until the last transaction on the date that is shown at the top of the first page."

The balance sheet is an elongation of the fundamental accounting equation, Assets = Liabilities + Proprietorship. If John Doe began a business by investing $10,000, the business would have an asset, Cash $10,000, and the business would be worth $10,000. If a balance sheet were made at this time, it would look like this:

Assets	=	Liabilities	+	Proprietorship
Cash $10,000		0	+	$10,000

If John Doe purchased merchandise amounting to $5,000 on credit, the balance sheet would be like this:

Assets	=	Liabilities	+	Proprietorship
Cash $10,000		Accounts		
Merchandise 5,000		Payable $5,000	+	$10,000
$15,000				

Can a person or business buy on credit and still be worth the same amount as the balance sheet indicates? Yes, but that does not mean that an individual, a family or a busi-

13

ness should buy on credit indiscriminately, because many assets decrease in value rapidly and as they decrease net worth decreases.

If one paid $2,000 on the account payable, his balance sheet would look like this:

	Assets	=	Liabilities	+	Proprietorship
Cash	$ 8,000		Accounts		
Merchandise	5,000		Payable $3,000	+	$10,000
	$13,000				

Does this mean that if a person or business pays its debts the business or person will be worth as much as before? Yes, the balance sheet is telling the truth. Then why don't people pay their debts promptly? Many people do. Some people have a particular fondness for the asset cash and like to keep it as long as they can. Since cash is the only asset that can ordinarily be used to pay debts (and sometimes it may not be available), the payment of debts is postponed temporarily.

From an accounting standpoint the reason that proprietorship did not change when the individual in the example above bought merchandise on credit is that assets and liabilities increased by the same amount, so nothing else could change. When he paid $2,000 on the account payable, the assets and liabilities decreased by the same amount, so nothing else could change.

When does proprietorship change? When a change in assets and liabilities is unequal. Suppose one sells $1,000 of merchandise for $2,000 cash. His balance sheet would be like this:

	Assets	=	Liabilities	+	Proprietorship
Cash	$10,000		Accounts		
Merchandise	4,000		Payable $3,000	+	$11,000
	$14,000				

If the firm to whom he owed the $3,000 accounts payable allowed him to discharge this obligation by paying them only $2,000, the balance sheet would be like this:

	Assets	=	Liabilities	+ Proprietorship
Cash	$ 8,000			
Merchandise	4,000		0	$12,000
	$12,000			

It is very important to remember that whenever there is an unequal change in assets and liabilities proprietorship will change.

For comparative purposes the assets are classified on a balance sheet into current and fixed. Current assets are cash and other assets that will turn into cash or be used up during the regular operations of a business in a short period of time, usually one year. In accounting, cash means any medium of exchange that banks will accept at face value for deposit. If it can be deposited in a bank without losing any of its face value, it's cash. Coins, paper money, checks and money orders are cash. Stamps are not cash. Accounts receivable is a current asset. It means that some commodity or service has been sold on credit, and since bills are supposed to be paid every month, they are current. Merchandise is current because it is being sold every day for cash or on account (which will soon be cash). Store supplies and office supplies are being used up constantly, so they are current.

Fixed assets are composed of the plant and equipment and are designated plant and equipment on many balance sheets. Assets that will not change to cash during the regular operations of a business in a short period of time are "fixed." Some of these are building, machinery, furniture and fixtures, and various kinds of equipment.

Current liabilities are those that should be paid in a short period of time, usually one year. These are accounts payable, notes payable within a year, interest payable, wages payable, and all debts that are to be paid within a year.

Fixed liabilities are labeled long-term debts by some

accountants and the terms are interchangeable. They include any debts that are not due within a year, such as mortgage payable, and bonds payable.

The current ratio is the ratio between current assets and current liabilities. This is also known as the working capital ratio. Bankers insist on a working capital ratio of at least two to one before making a loan. If a firm's current assets total $10,000 and its current liabilities total $5,000, it would theoretically be capable of repaying a loan of $5,000 during a year's time because it should realize approximately $10,000 cash from its assets and have to pay out only $5,000 in cash on its liabilities. An example of a classified balance sheet follows.

ACME CLEANERS

Balance Sheet

December 31, 19—

Current Assets:		
Cash	$10,000	
Merchandise	12,000	
Accounts Receivable	8,000	
Prepaid Rent	2,400	
Store Supplies	600	
Total Current Assets		$33,000
Fixed Assets:		
Building	$20,000	
Land	10,000	
Equipment	10,000	
Total Fixed Assets		40,000
Total Assets		$73,000

Current Liabilities:		
Accounts Payable	$10,000	
Wages Payable	2,000	
Total Current Liabilities		$12,000
Fixed Liabilities:		
Mortgage Payable	$10,000	
Notes Payable (5 yrs.)	8,000	
Total Fixed Liabilities		$18,000
Total Liabilities		$30,000
Net Worth		
John Doe, Proprietorship		43,000
Total Liabilities and Proprietorship		$73,000

This type of balance sheet in which the assets are listed on the left side of the page and the liabilities are listed on the right side of the page is known as the account form. Balance sheets are also made in a report form, with the assets listed at the top of the page and the liabilities and proprietorship listed below the assets.

The profit or loss of a business for a period of time can be determined by a comparison of balance sheets. If a balance sheet prepared for Acme Cleaners a year ago had shown John Doe's proprietorship to be $23,000, this would mean that this year's profit was $20,000 if John Doe had not invested or withdrawn any assets from the business. If the proprietorship had increased by $20,000 during the year and the proprietor had withdrawn $5,000 during the year, the profit would have been $25,000. If a person can take $5,000 from a business and the business is still worth $20,000 more at the end of a year than it was at the beginning, the business must have made a $25,000 profit. If, instead of withdrawing $5,000 from the business, the proprietor had invested $5,000 and at the end of the year his proprietorship had increased by $20,000, his profit would have been $15,000 because he did not make the $5,000; he put it in himself.

Suppose someone prepares a balance sheet on December 31, 1974, and finds his proprietorship to be $20,000. On December 31, 1975, he prepares another balance sheet and finds that his proprietorship has increased to $40,000. He has invested $10,000 in the business during the year and he has withdrawn $5,000. How much profit has he made during the year? A good way to determine the profit is to find out how much the proprietorship would have been on December 31, 1975, if there had been no profit at all. This is easy to do. The proprietorship was $20,000 at the beginning. The owner invested $10,000 in the business which would make the proprietorship $30,000. He withdrew $5,000 from the business during the year which would make the proprietorship $25,000 if there had been no profit. The ending

proprietorship was $40,000, so he must have made
$15,000. Any time anyone wishes to determine the profit
for a period he can do so by comparing the beginning
and ending proprietorships and taking into consideration
the withdrawals and additional investments. This will
serve as a double check in preparing a profit and loss
statement. If the profit is determined to be a certain
amount by comparing balance sheets, and then one gets
the same profit after preparing a profit and loss statement (Chapter III), he can feel confident that the profit
is correct.

Chapter III

THE PROFIT AND LOSS STATEMENT

THE PURPOSE of the profit and loss statement (or
income statement) is to explain why the proprietorship of a business changed during a period of
time. Accountants do not prepare the statement to determine the amount of the profit or the loss because
that is usually known before the statement is prepared.
As was explained in the previous chapter, the amount
of the profit or the loss can be determined by comparing
two balance sheets. How to prepare a work sheet is
explained in chapter VI, and the amount of the profit
or loss is shown on the work sheet. The work sheet is
prepared before the statements are prepared.

The Internal Revenue Service will not allow an explanation of the amount of profit for a year by showing
the difference between ending and beginning proprietorship. This is a fine check on profit but they want more
detail. Internal Revenue says to list income and list
expenses and in that manner explain net profit. Schedule

"C" of the income tax return is in the form of a profit and loss statement.

A fiscal period is the length of time covered by a profit and loss statement. It may be a month, a quarter, a year or any period of time. For that reason the heading of a profit and loss statement differs a bit from the heading of a balance sheet. On a balance sheet was listed the firm's name, the name of the statement and the date. The heading of a profit and loss statement will be as follows:

ACME CLEANERS
Profit and Loss Statement
For the year ending December 31, 19__

The heading must cover a fiscal period and must plainly state whether it is a month, a quarter or whatever period of time it represents. The statement would have little meaning if it did not cover a period of time. For instance, a profit of $5,000 may be good for a month but it may be very bad for a year.

For comparative purposes the expenses are usually classified on a profit and loss statement into at least two categories—selling and general. There can be more classifications, but there should be at least these two. If an expense is closely related to selling, such as salesmen's salaries and advertising, it should be listed as selling. If it is a more general type of expense, such as rent or office salaries, it should be listed as general. A profit and loss statement for a small cleaning establishment follows:

ACME CLEANERS
Profit and Loss Statement
For the month ending January 31, 19___

Income:			
Cleaning Income			$10,000
Expenses:			
Selling Expenses:			
Delivery Expense		$1,000	
Advertising		500	
Sales Salaries		1,500	
Total Selling Expenses		$3,000	
General Expenses:			
Laundry Supply Expenses		$1,000	
Rent Expense		1,000	
Office Salaries		1,000	
Total General Expenses		$3,000	
Total Expenses			6,000
Net Profit (or net income)			$4,000

To classify a selling expense as a general expense would not change the net profit, as the total expenses would still be the same. Occasionally it is difficult to classify expenses with certainty, and accountants can disagree on expense classification without affecting the validity of the statement.

There is a very close relationship between the balance sheet and the profit and loss statement. In the final analysis the latter statement is really a part of the former. A balance sheet could be prepared with all the information that goes on a profit and loss statement included in the proprietorship section. However, this would make the balance sheet unwieldy, so it is best for the information in a profit and loss statement to be shown separately. A profit or loss statement for a service business, such as a laundry, dry cleaner, doctor, auctioneer or accountant, is simpler than one for a mercantile business, because a business that is selling goods or products has to determine the cost of the goods that have been sold. This adds a section to the profit and loss statement entitled "cost of goods sold" or "cost of sales." This section will be explained in chapter XIII, which deals with a mercantile business.

Chapter IV

DEBITUS AND CREDITUS

In Brief

The Owner, or the Owing thing,
or whatsoever come to thee:
upon the Left hand see thou bring
for there the same must placed be.

But—

they unto whom thou doest owe
upon the Right let them be set;
or whatsoe'er doth from thee go
to place them there do not forget.[1]

[1] *The Romance of the Ledger* (A brochure prepared by the Remington Rand Business Service. Used by permission.)

TWO HUNDRED years ago accountants sang poems such as the one above to help them record the proper debits and credits. This is a very fine rule for the theory of debit and credit, but in two hundred years an easier way should have been found to explain it. Debit means enter on the left side of an account and credit means enter on the right side. In double entry accounting there is a debit and a credit entry for each business transaction that is to be recorded. There may be more than one debit or more than one credit, but the total of each side must be the same. The terms "charge" and "debit" are synonymous. Many people have used the term charge without knowing exactly what it meant. When they bought something at the store and said, "Charge it," they were telling the merchant to enter the amount on the left side of their account. When they paid something on the bill and said, "Give me credit for this," they were saying to enter the amount on the right side of their account.

A general ledger account has a left and a right side and a place for dates as in the illustration that follows.

CASH   Account No. 1

Date	Items	Posting Reference	Debit	Date	Items	Posting Reference	Credit
Jan. 1		1	$2,000-	Jan. 15 20			$500- 500-

"T" accounts are used in illustrations and problems because they can be drawn quickly and are real time-savers. A "T" account follows. It gets its name because of its similarity to that letter.

CASH

$2,000-	$500-
	500-

A group of accounts is called a ledger. The accounts in the ledger are usually arranged to correspond to their classifications on the balance sheet and profit and loss statements. Current assets are grouped together, for instance. However, a ledger can be arranged in any order that the person keeping it wants.

One should never attempt to memorize the theory of debit and credit. Nor should one try to commit to memory the following: debits increase assets and expenses, decrease liabilities and proprietorship; credits decrease assets and expenses, increase liabilities, proprietorship and income. Memory is too fickle. All that has to be remembered is something that is already known—THE FUNDAMENTAL ACCOUNTING EQUATION:

Assets   =   Liabilities   +   Proprietorship

To increase an account, one enters on the side of the equation that the account is on. Assets are on the left of the equation, so to increase an asset it should be recorded on the left. Liabilities and proprietorship are on the right of the equality sign, so to increase them they should be (credited) recorded on the right.

Fortunately, an account has only two sides. If one knows how to increase an account, how would he decrease one? By entering on the other side, of course! Some transactions for John Doe follow in order to illustrate how easy it is to determine the debit and credit. John Doe begins a laundry business by investing $10,000 cash. Cash is an asset and the business has more of it, so he will debit cash to increase it because assets are on the left side of the equation. For every debit there must be a credit, so he will credit John Doe, Proprietorship, so that the ledger will be in balance.

CASH	John Doe, Proprietorship
$10,000			$10,000

Other than making equal debits and credits why did he credit the proprietorship account? Because proprietorship is on the right side of the equation and to increase it he entered the amount on the right side.

Suppose John Doe buys $1,000 worth of laundry supplies and pays cash. Most people understand the cash account better than any other, so the entry to the cash account should be determined first. If John Doe spends $1,000, he has $1,000 less. How does he decrease cash? It is an asset on the left of the equation, so to increase it he enters on the left. To decrease it he must enter on the other side, so he will credit cash. He will debit laundry supplies because it is an asset and it is increased. John Doe buys laundry equipment on credit. Laundry equipment is an asset and John Doe has more of it, so he enters on the left to increase. Accounts payable is a liability and Doe's liability is increased, so he enters on the right.

The word debit means only that it is entered on the left. It increases some accounts and decreases some. Credit means only that it is entered on the right side. It increases some accounts and decreases some. One can always tell which it does by constantly bearing in mind the fundamental accounting equation.

It probably has been noticed by now that only balance sheet accounts have been used in the transactions recorded. What about profit and loss accounts? A profit and loss statement has to be prepared too. Expense and income accounts are temporary proprietorship accounts. They are open during a fiscal year so that a profit and loss statement can be prepared. In the final analysis they are proprietorship accounts, so that is the clue. Do expenses make John Doe worth more or less? Less, of course. How does he decrease proprietorship? By entering on the left, so expenses are debited because expenses decrease proprietorship. Suppose John Doe pays a wages expense of $100. The entry would have been determined by the debit or credit to cash, but assume the entry to the expense is to be determined first. Expenses make the proprietor worth less. Debits decrease proprietorship, so the expense is debited.

If the John Doe Laundry performs laundry services for customers on credit amounting to $500, he would debit accounts receivable to increase the asset and he would credit laundry income because income makes the proprietor worth more.

Remember, an account is increased by making an entry on the side of the accounting equation that it is on, and that assets, liabilities and proprietorship are the only real accounts. They are the only ones that remain on and on. The others are temporary proprietorship accounts and are closed each year; they will be discussed in a later chapter.

The International Business Machines slogan comes in handy here.

THINK!

| Assets | = | Liabilities | + | Proprietorship |
| Left increases | | | Right increases | |

An account has only two sides, so all that has to be remembered is how to increase them.

Periodically, and certainly at least once a year, a trial balance is taken to see if the accounts with debit balances equal the accounts with credit balances. If all the debits in an account total $2,000 and all the credits total $1,000, the account is said to have a debit balance of $1,000. The balances of all the accounts in the ledger are listed and totaled in this manner.

Cash	$10,000	
Supplies	8,000	
Accounts Payable		$ 4,000
Proprietorship		3,000
Laundry Income		12,000
Expenses	1,000	
Totals	$19,000	$19,000

An accountant has two strikes against him as far as the trial balance is concerned. If it balances, he may be right and he may be wrong. If it does not balance, he is wrong. In the trial balance illustrated, any of the debit or credit balances could be switched around and still total $19,000, but it would then be incorrect. A trial balance proves that the debits and credits are equal, nothing else.

Chapter V

THE JOURNAL

AN ACCOUNT is a classifying and summarizing device, so the information that it contains is meager. Original entries are first recorded in a journal which is known as a book of original entry. The first journal that is introduced in accounting is usually a general journal. This is a two-column journal with a place for the date, a place in which to write the name of the accounts to be debited and credited, and a posting reference column. Posting means transferring debits and credits from a journal to a ledger.

Date		Description	Posting Reference	Debit	Credit
19__					
Jan.	1	Cash	1	$10,000	
		John Doe, Proprietor	4		$10,000
		To record investment			
"	5	Laundry Supplies	2	2,000	
		Accounts Payable	3		2,000
		Purchased laundry supplies on account			
"	10	Cash	1	4,000	
		Laundry Income	5		4,000
		To record cash income from services			

```
        Cash        #1          Laundry Supplies   #2
  J1  $10,000 |                 J1  $2,000 |
  J1    4,000 |                            |

  Accounts Payable  #3      John Doe, Proprietor  #4
            | $2,000 J1                | $10,000 J1

                Laundry Income     #5
                        | $4,000 J1
```

In the previous illustration a few familiar transactions have been first recorded in a journal. If it can be determined which accounts are to be debited and credited, it is easy to record these debits and credits in the journal. In the first transaction John Doe began a laundry business with a cash investment of $10,000. The fundamental accounting equation is used to determine which accounts to debit and which to credit. The next transaction recorded was the purchase of laundry supplies on account, and the next one recorded the cash taken in from laundry sales. After these transactions were recorded in the journal, the debits and credits were transferred to the ledger which is illustrated next. All the accounts in the ledger have a number. Since the cash account is number "1," a "1" was placed in the posting reference column to show the number of the account to which the amount was posted. The $10,000 debit to the cash account came from the first page of the journal, so "J1" is placed in the posting reference column of the account to show from whence it came.

An accountant should be able to trace any debit or credit from the journal to the ledger. He should also be able to trace any debit or credit from the ledger to the journal. This helps him to locate errors and it also helps an auditor or anyone who might check the records.

Actually one may not be able to see that the journal is going to be of any great help in accounting at this stage. If he does not see the value of a general journal, he certainly will see the value of special journals which will be introduced later. Since the general journal is the simplest, it is usually the first one introduced. It is good to learn how to record in and post from a general journal because this principle will always be used in accounting.

Chapter VI

THE WORK SHEET—IT'S WONDERFUL

ONE OF THE FIRST things learned in the study of accounting is the preparation of a balance sheet and a profit and loss statement. The theory of debit and credit is learned early so that a trial balance may be prepared. Even though the trial balance is correct it soon becomes evident that some of the amounts on the trial balance must be changed and some account balances must be added if the balance sheet and profit and loss statements are to reflect the actual operations of a business. Some supplies have been used and some are still on hand. Some prepaid rent has expired. The business may have debts that it owes, such as wages or utilities that have not been recorded. Debts owed to the business, such as interest or rent may not have been recorded.

Actually, the preparation of the statements under these circumstances becomes complicated. Some of the account balances on the trial balance can be used as they are, but some cannot. The accountant must combine the trial balance with "supplementary data." This supplementary data contains the inventories, the payables, receivables, and any other information not furnished by the trial balance.

A device that allows one to gather together on one sheet of paper all the information that he needs for the preparation of the statements is called the work sheet. It truly is a marvelous device. It is as much an accountant's tool as is an adding machine. However, it is not part of the accounting records. The accountant does not necessarily show it to anyone, but he knows its value, and few accountants would be without it. It is worth learning about just for its value in the preparation of the statements, although it has many more uses. One will find that when he has completed a work sheet correctly he knows that he can complete the remaining steps in what is known as the "accounting cycle" and be ready to start over again on another fiscal period. Without the work sheet it would be most difficult to learn the remaining steps in the accounting cycle. With it, it will be easy.

Listed on page 31 is a trial balance of the Acme Laundry, John Doe, Proprietor.

ACME LAUNDRY

Trial Balance

December 31, 19__

Cash	$ 5,000	
Laundry Supplies	2,000	
Accounts Payable		$ 5,000
Accounts Receivable	4,000	
Prepaid Rent	3,600	
Wages Expense	5,000	
Laundry Income		11,000
J. Doe, Proprietor		3,600
	$19,600	$19,600

Although this trial balance is correct, some of the accounts on it are incorrect and have to be changed or adjusted before the statements are made. Doe bought $2,000 of laundry supplies, but he has been using some and now, after counting it, he finds that he has only $500 of laundry supplies on hand. The rent was paid in advance for three years and this fiscal period is one year. Part of the $3,600 is expense and part asset. John Doe owes $500 for wages and the liability is not on the trial balance. Wages expense must be $500 more however, and the liability must be reported on the balance sheet. All this information is gathered together on a work sheet (see page 32).

The Acme Laundry trial balance was placed on the work sheet in the first two columns. Because John Doe had only $500 of laundry supplies on hand, $1,500 of supplies had to be subtracted from the $2,000 that was on the trial balance. Laundry supplies is a debit, so in order to subtract, the $1,500 had to be a credit. For every credit there must be a debit, so something must be charged with $1,500. A suitable name was chosen. If John Doe bought $2,000 of laundry supplies and all but $500 of it is gone, we assume that he used it in the business. Laundry Supplies Used or Laundry Supplies Expense describes the account nicely and either name is acceptable.

ACME CLEANERS

Work Sheet

For year ending December 31, 19—

adjusting entries
accts to be closed

Account No.	Name of Account	Trial Balance Debit	Trial Balance Credit	Adjustments Debit	Adjustments Credit	Profit and Loss Debit	Profit and Loss Credit	Balance Sheet Debit	Balance Sheet Credit
1	Cash	$ 5,000						$ 5,000	
5	Laundry Supplies	2,000			$1,500			500	
7	Accounts Payable		$ 5,000						$ 5,000
3	Accounts Receivable	4,000						4,000	
4	Prepaid Rent	3,600			1,200			2,400	
8	Wages Expense	5,000		$ 500		$ 5,500			
9	Laundry Income		11,000				$11,000		
10	J. Doe, Prop.		3,600						3,600
		$19,600	$19,600						
	Laundry Supplies Expense			1,500		1,500			
	Rent Expense			1,200		1,200			
	Wages Payable				500				500
				$3,200	$3,200	8,200	11,000	11,900	9,100
	Net Profit					2,800			2,800
						$11,000	$11,000	$11,900	$11,900

32

John Doe paid $3,600 for three years' rent which is $1,200 a year, of course. After one year, Doe's expense is $1,200 and his asset, Prepaid Rent, must be $2,400. His asset, Prepaid Rent, is reduced to $2,400 by a credit of $1,200. The one year's rent expense of $1,200 is charged to Rent Expense which describes the expense perfectly.

Doe's laundry owed $500 for wages at the end of the year. Even though this has not been paid it must be included in the expenses for 1968. All liabilities must be shown on the balance sheet. Doe adds $500 to his wages by a debit and records his liability, Wages Payable, by a credit of $500.

An adjusted trial balance has been omitted purposely, because by the time the adjusted trial balance is finished, almost enough time has been used to have completed the entire work sheet. It serves little if any purpose, and one usually realizes this after preparing it a few times and omits the adjusted trial balance from future work sheets. After the adjustments have been made, it becomes a matter of sorting the accounts into the profit and loss columns and the balance sheet columns. One should begin with the first account, Cash, and place the amount where it belongs. It may be checked, if desired, to make sure that none is omitted. Each account down the trial balance should be entered in its proper place. No attempt should be made to try to pick out the profit and loss accounts and then the balance sheet accounts because an account is apt to be omitted. The difference between the profit and loss columns and the balance sheet columns will be the same and on opposite sides. In this illustration $2,800 was added to the left side of profit and loss to make it balance, so the same amount must be added to the right side of the balance sheet columns to make it balance.

The $2,800 represents net profit because the right side, the income side, is greater than the left or expense side. Profits increase proprietorship, so it is added to the right side of the balance sheet columns.

The work sheet, marvelous as it is, is not magic. One still has to know whether an account is a profit and loss account or a balance sheet account. This is illustrated by the following:

2	4	2			4
1	2		2	1	
5	6	5	6		
6	5		5	6	
4	3	4			3
3	1	3			1
21	21	14	13	7	8
			1	1	
		14	14	8	8

When two columns of accounts are in balance and they are separated into four columns of accounts, keeping debits debits and credits credits, the difference between the new columns will be the same and on opposite sides. As long as the left numbers are placed on the left and the right numbers are placed on the right the difference will be the same and on opposite sides. The little trial balance should balance at an odd figure so the difference between the two sides will not be zero. No one should ask the question, "My work sheet balanced all the way across the bottom so why isn't it correct?" In the little work sheet just pictured, nothing was said about profit and loss and balance sheet columns. They were mixed up any way anyone wanted them. If some profit and loss items are included in the balance sheet and vice versa, it will balance across the bottom of the work sheet. The work sheet is a wonderful device, but it will not prepare itself.

On a work sheet it makes no difference whether the balance sheet or the profit and loss columns come first. Customarily the profit and loss columns are first. If many of them are prepared, profit and loss and the balance sheet columns may be switched to break the monotony.

Chapter VII

ADJUSTING ENTRIES

AFTER THE WORK SHEET is prepared, the statements are made from the information on the work sheet. Management or owners are very anxious to see these statements. Accountants cannot offer management the work sheet and inform them that all the information is on it. Laymen could get very little from the work sheet, so the profit and loss statement and the balance sheet are prepared in such a manner that anyone could understand them.

After the statements are prepared, the accountant is ready to go to work. Anyone reading the statements he has prepared assumes that he has taken the figures from his ledger. They also take for granted that he can prove any of the ledger figures by referring to journals. At the time the work sheet is completed and the statements made the accountant knows that he has used many figures on the statements that are not in his ledger. He knows that he may even have used some accounts that are not in the ledger. For a large business there would be numerous amounts in the statements that would not be in the ledger. What amounts or accounts would be in the statements that would not be in the ledger? Those that were added to the trial balance or changed in the adjustment columns. In the work sheet in the previous chapter John Doe changed the laundry supplies amount, added the laundry supplies expense account, changed the prepaid rent amount, added the rent expense account, changed the wages expense amount and added the wages payable account. None of this information would be in his ledger although he has included this information in the statements.

To make ledgers agree with statements, journal entries are prepared and posted. This results in ledgers that agree with the statements. The information needed for these entries is gathered together in two columns on the work sheet, so this "fine device" may be used again.

Date	Description	Posting Reference	Debit	Credit
	Adjusting Entries			
19—				
Dec. 31	Laundry Supplies Expense	11	$1,500	
	Laundry Supplies	5		$1,500
31	Rent Expense	12	1,200	
	Prepaid Rent	4		1,200
31	Wages Expense	8	500	
	Wages Payable	7		500

In the example, the adjusting entries have been labeled as such. The two words may be underscored for emphasis. This enables anyone to know that these are not original entries. The debits and credits are not copied from the top of the work sheet to the bottom in that order. The end result would be the same, but it would be more difficult to explain. One should begin at the top of the adjustment columns of the work sheet and come down to the first debit or credit. The corresponding debit or credit should be located and recorded. It is customary in any general journal entry to record the debit first. The remaining debits and credits are recorded in order. After these entries have been posted, the ledger accounts and amounts will agree with the statements.

Chapter VIII

CLOSING ENTRIES

AFTER RECORDING AND POSTING the adjusting entries, the next step in the accounting cycle, or the work at the close of the fiscal period, is the recording and posting of the closing entries.

Many accounts are closed at the end of the fiscal year. This is done to make things easier for the accountant in the following year. All the temporary proprietorship accounts are closed. Any account that is used in determining the profit or loss for a year should be closed, because it is easier to determine the profit or loss for the next year if the accountant can begin the year with a clean slate, no expense and no income. It would be a terrible ordeal for bookkeepers and accountants if the sales account contained thirty years of sales and the various expense accounts contained thirty years of expenses and the figures for one year had to be chosen. It is more logical to let each year be a fiscal period unto itself with no income and no expense at the beginning. This is done by means of closing entries.

Thanks to that wonderful device, the work sheet, all the accounts that have to be closed are grouped together in two columns, the profit and loss columns.

Date	Description	Posting Ref.	Debit	Credit
19—	*Closing Entries*			
Dec. 31	Laundry Income	9	$11,000	
	Profit and Loss Summary	20		$11,000
31	Profit and Loss Summary	20	8,200	
	Wages Expense	8		5,500
	Laundry Supplies Expense	11		1,500
	Rent Expense	12		1,200
31	Profit and Loss Summary	20	2,800	
	John Doe, Proprietor	10		2,800

Since debits are recorded first in general journal entries, the income accounts are customarily closed first. In referring to John Doe's Acme Laundry work sheet it is seen that the only income account is laundry income, so laundry income is debited and an account, profit and loss summary, is credited. This is a temporary account that may have some other name, such as income summary, because it is only open for a short period of time. It is used in order not to clutter up the proprietorship account which stays open all the time. The expenses are closed next. One could debit profit and loss summary for each expense, but it is quicker to use the total which is on the work sheet. After each expense is credited, the profit and loss summary account should be closed. The balance of the account is $2,800 as indicated by the work sheet and it is a credit balance. Profit and loss summary is closed by a debit and John Doe, proprietorship is credited.

Had John Doe withdrawn any cash from the business it may have been recorded by a debit to John Doe, Drawing instead of John Doe, Proprietorship. If this had been done, the drawing account would have been in the balance sheet columns. This account does not have to be closed since it is a balance sheet item. Custom dictates that it be closed unless the accountant is otherwise instructed. If it is to be closed, it should be closed directly into the proprietorship account.

If John Doe had withdrawn $500 from his laundry business, his drawing, proprietorship, and profit and loss summary accounts just before the final closing entries would appear as follows:

Profit & Loss Summary	J. Doe, Prop.	J. Doe, Drawing
$8,200 | $11,000	500 | $2,800	$500 | 500

Profit and Loss Summary is debited with $2,800 and J. Doe, Proprietor is credited with $2,800. To close J. Doe, Drawing, J. Doe, Proprietorship is debited and J. Doe, Drawing is credited. Some close the summary account into the drawing account and then close the balance of the drawing account into the capital account. Others close the drawing account into the summary account and then close the balance of the summary account into the capital account. Either way gets the same result, but the latter two are a little slower due to the arithmetic involved. In corporations there are no drawing accounts and the summary account is closed directly into a surplus or retained earnings account.

Chapter IX

THE POST-CLOSING TRIAL BALANCE

AFTER THE CLOSING ENTRIES the next step in the accounting cycle is the preparation of a post-closing trial balance.

The work at the close of the fiscal year is begun by preparing a trial balance and placing it on the first two columns of a work sheet. Now, several steps later, a trial balance is made again. Isn't that overdoing it a little? It may seem so, but many entries have been recorded in the ledger since that first trial balance was prepared. In the small illustration that has been used it may not seem to be many, but in a representative business there would be many more adjusting entries and many more closing entries. The fact that the ledger was in balance when the work was begun at the close of the fiscal year does not mean that the ledger is still in balance after these additional postings have been made. In posting it is very easy to transpose a figure, recording $617.43 as $671.43. No one would want to wait an entire year or even a month to find out if his ledger was in balance after closing. A post-closing trial balance is prepared so that there can be no concern about the ledger being in balance.

The post-closing trial balance is prepared by recording the balance of each account from each ledger page, beginning with page one, which is usually the cash account. If time is at a premium, it can be prepared much more quickly by copying it from the last two columns of the work sheet. The net profit must be added to the proprietorship. The total at which the post-closing trial balance will balance is already on the work sheet unless there is a drawing account. If there is a drawing account, the amount in the account is subtracted from the proprietorship and also subtracted from the total. After a post-closing trial balance is prepared in the regular way it can be checked with the last two columns on the work sheet for accuracy.

The accounts on the post-closing trial balance represent the "real" accounts, since they remain open indefinitely. A real account is a balance sheet account. The temporary proprietorship accounts that are closed are referred to as nominal accounts.

Chapter X

SPECIAL JOURNALS: THE SALES AND SALES RETURNS

THE INCOME ACCOUNT for a mercantile or merchandising business is usually termed sales.

As a business grows, it finds itself in need of faster and better ways to record transactions. Any bookkeeper who continually recorded the same type of transaction in a general journal would certainly begin to wonder if there were not an easier way to do it. One such transaction would be sales of merchandise to customers on credit. When a sale is made to a customer on account, the most important thing to record is the customer's name. The amount would come next in importance. To expedite the recording of the customers' names, an account with each customer should be kept in a separate ledger. The names should be kept in alphabetical order for quick and easy reference in case a customer asks for the balance of his account. Ledgers that are kept apart from the general ledger are called subsidiary ledgers. Each subsidiary ledger should have a descriptive title, so a good name for this one is "accounts receivable." Since all the customers' names are kept in a separate ledger, the general ledger does not balance unless something is recorded in it to take the place of all the names. This is done by means of a controlling account which is called accounts receivable. An illustration of how credit sales would be recorded in a general journal and posted to the subsidiary ledger and to the general ledger follows.

Date	Description	Posting Ref.	Debit	Credit
June 1	Accounts Receivable—J. Jones	23/√	$1,000	
	Sales			$1,000
2	Accounts Receivable—H. Brown	23/√	2,000	
	Sales			2,000
3	Accounts Receivable—W. Harris	23/√	2,500	
	Sales			2,500

GENERAL LEDGER   ACCOUNTS RECEIVABLE LEDGER

Accounts Receivable #23   Brown, Henry
       $1,000 $2,000 |
        2,000
        2,500   Harris, Will
                                    $2,500 |

       Sales #27
        $1,000
         2,000   Jones, John
         2,500 $1,000 |

If the preceding illustration were on a blackboard, it would be very easy to demonstrate that a special sales journal would save much time and space. The journal would be labeled sales journal after all of the general journal had been erased but the following:

Sales Journal

Date	Name	Posting Reference	Amount
19—			
June 1	John Jones	√	$1,000
2	Henry Brown	√	2,000
3	Will Harris	√	2,500
		23/27	$5,500

GENERAL LEDGER	ACCOUNTS RECEIVABLE LEDGER

Accounts Receivable #23

SJ1 $5,500 |

Brown, Henry

$2,000 |

Harris, Will

$2,500 |

Sales   #27

$5,500 SJ1

Jones, John

$1,000 |

As for the space saved, it can be seen that over one-half of the general journal has been eliminated. As for the time saved, it may not seem like much when limited to the three transactions in the illustration, but suppose there were three hundred sales on credit, or even three thousand. By having a special journal used only for credit sales an accountant or bookkeeper can total the sales and post only one debit and one credit to the general ledger instead of three hundred or three thousand as would have to be done if he recorded these transactions in the general journal.

The sales journal does not save any time so far as the subsidiary ledger is concerned. Each debit and credit must be posted to each customer's account. This is done daily, however, so that it will not be such a great task at the end of the month when it is time to send out the bills. Posting to subsidiary ledgers is constantly going on whenever time is available. As each amount is posted, it is checked off with a check mark. The numbers "23" and "27" indicate that the amount of $5,500 has been posted to these accounts. If the posting reference column is cramped for space, these numbers may be written under the total in parenthesis. It is very important to keep up-to-date in posting to subsidiary ledgers. If a customer wants to know the amount he owes, someone should be able to get him that information immediately. He should be asked if he has purchased anything on credit that day. If he has, it should be added to his balance and the information given to him. It would be bad public relations if a customer asked the amount he owed and was told to wait fifteen or twenty minutes while his account was posted. Some businesses use an account for subsidiary ledgers—debit column, credit column and balance column. This type of a subsidiary ledger account is illustrated below.

Date		Posting Reference	Debit	Credit	Balance

Small business establishments use a special sales journal. For large businesses even this time-saver is too slow. Almost any business prepares a sales ticket when merchandise is sold on account. Either sales ticket books with a carbon sheet or a machine that keeps a roll of tickets inside are used. In either case one copy is usually given to the customer. If these sales tickets are numerous the posting to the Accounts Receivable ledger should be done from them because they contain all the information needed. They should contain the date, the customer's name, his address, the amount of the sale and the terms. Since the subsidiary ledger is in alphabetical order, it is a simple matter to transfer this information to the accounts in the ledger. All anyone needs to know is the alphabet, and his left hand from his right.

After the tickets have been posted to the subsidiary ledger, they should be added on a printing calculator and given to the person in charge of the general journal. He would then make an entry such as the following:

Date		Posting Reference	Debit	Credit
19__				
June 30	Accounts Receivable	23	$150,000	
	Sales	27		$150,000

This entry would only have to be made once a month or whenever a trial balance was desired.

Occasionally a sale is made and the merchandise is not to the customers liking and he returns it for credit. At other times the goods may be soiled or damaged in some manner and he is given an allowance. These transactions are recorded in an account called "sales returns and allowances." If these returns are infrequent, no special journal is needed, and that old reliable, the general journal is used to record the transactions.

Date	Description	Posting Reference	Debit	Credit
19__	Sales Returns and Allowances		$100	
Mar. 5	Accounts Receivable—J. Jones			$100

When the merchandise is returned, the customer expects credit for it and this is done by crediting his account in the subsidiary ledger and by crediting the controlling account, Accounts Receivable, in the general ledger. Since that is the reverse of the original entry, it may seem that the credit should be reversed and the debit to the sales account reversed. The reason this is not done is that businessmen want this important information to show up on the profit and loss statement. A profit and loss statement like this:

Sales		$70,000
Less:	Sales Returns and Allowances	6,000
		$64,000

gives more information than one like this:

Sales	$64,000

Both statements would show the same profit of course; but, the fact that customers are bringing merchandise back or that it is damaged is information that should be reported on the statement.

This may influence purchasing policies in the future. The sales returns and allowances account is classified as a minus income account.

If there are many returns, a journal like the sales journal should be used.

Sales Returns and Allowances Journal

Date	Name	Posting Reference	Amount
19__			
June 10	John Jones	√	$100
15	Will Harris	√	125
		28/23	$225

The posting would be almost the opposite of the sales journal. In the general ledger account number 28, Sales Returns and Allowances, would be debited, and account number 23, Accounts Receivable, would be credited. Jones and Harris would be credited with $100 and $125, respectively, in the accounts receivable ledger.

Chapter XI

SPECIAL JOURNALS: PURCHASES AND PURCHASES RETURNS

AS A BUSINESS EXPANDS it should be looking for easier and quicker ways of recording its purchases of merchandise. All merchandise purchased on account could be recorded in a one-column purchase journal similar to the sales journal. The subsidiary ledger should be called the accounts payable ledger.

Purchases Journal

Date	Name	Posting Reference	Amount
19__			
April 1	Acme Company	√	$2,000
9	Ajax Corporation	√	3,000
		29/3	$5,000

GENERAL LEDGER   ACCOUNTS PAYABLE LEDGER

Purchases #29	
PJ1 $5,000	

Acme Company	
	$2,000

Accounts Payable #3	
	$5,000 PJ1

Ajax Corporation	
	$3,000

If there were many returns of merchandise, a one-column purchases returns and allowances journal should be used. The total would be debited to Accounts Payable and credited to Purchases Returns and Allowances in the general ledger. Accounts in the subsidiary ledger would be debited for the amount of the returns.

The purchase returns and allowances account is a minus cost account and is deducted from purchases in the cost section of the profit and loss statement.

Mercantile businesses purchase almost everything from wholesalers on credit, not only the merchandise which they intend to sell, but store supplies, office supplies and items which they intend to use themselves. When merchandise is purchased, the account charged is Purchases. When anything else is purchased the account charged is one that describes the purchase, such as "store supplies." If a purchases journal is used, one is usually designed in which all purchases on credit can be recorded.

In designing a multi-column journal such as the one shown on page 47, special columns should be used for those items that are purchased frequently. For the journal to function properly, however, it must be designed so that any credit purchase can be recorded in it no matter how infrequent the purchase. This is accomplished by using the general column usually on the extreme right of the journal. If enough column headings were put in to enable one to record anything that might ever be purchased on credit, the journal would have to be several feet in width.

PURCHASES JOURNAL

Date	Purchased from	Posting Reference	Accounts Payable Credit	Purchases Debit	Store Supplies Debit	Office Supplies Debit	General Accounts	Posting Reference	Debit
19— Oct.									
1	Acme Company		$2,000	$2,000					
3	General Supply Co.		500		$500				
9	Office Supply Inc.		300			$300			
9	Ajax Corp.		3,000	3,000					
12	Ray, Inc.		1,000				Store Equipment	37	$1,000
15	Gen. Supply Co.		200		200				
19	Office Supply Inc.		100			100			
30	Wilcox, Inc.		900				Office Equipment	39	900
			$8,000	$5,000	$700	$400			$1,900
			(3)	(29)	(31)	(33)			(√)

49

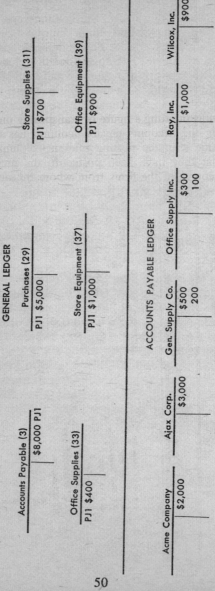

Before posting the journal the columns are totaled. This, or any other multi-column journal, should be "proved" before it is posted. This is done by adding the debit columns and by adding the credit columns and comparing the totals. If they do not equal each other, the error should be found before posting is begun. If a ledger is ever out of balance, it should only be due to carelessness, such as omitting a figure or transposing one. Each number in the accounts payable column has a check mark beside it in the posting reference column. This means that they have been posted to the credit side of the accounts of the firms from whom the purchases were made. These names are in the accounts payable ledger. The total of the accounts payable has been posted to the credit side of account number 3. Purchases of $5,000 have been debited to account number 29. Store Supplies of $700 have been debited to account number 31. Store Equipment has been debited to account number 37 as indicated by the posting reference column for the general accounts, and Office Equipment has been debited to account number 39 as indicated in the same column. The total of the general debits, $1,900, has been checked off to make sure it is posted nowhere. The only reason it was added was to prove the journal.

As in recording credit sales from sales tickets, large firms post to the accounts payable ledger from the invoices received from their suppliers. These are then totaled on a printing calculator and a general journal entry made, such as this:

Date	Description	Posting Reference	Debit	Credit
19__				
Oct. 30	Purchases	29	$5,000	
	Store Supplies	31	700	
	Office Supplies	33	400	
	Store Equipment	37	1,000	
	Office Equipment	39	900	
	Accounts Payable	3		$8,000

Actually, small firms with little office help should not record credit purchases at all. Much time and effort would be saved if they would only wait until the first of the month and record the purchases when they paid their bills. This would eliminate four entries, a debit and a credit to Accounts Payable and a debit and a credit to the creditor's account in the subsidiary ledger. Unpaid invoices should be filed and compared with the bill when it is received at the first of the month. If they agree, a check should be written and the account paid and recorded. This would result in a debit to Purchases and a credit to Cash instead of a debit to Purchases and a credit to Accounts Payable and a credit to the creditor's account and a debit to Accounts Payable and a credit to Cash. The only time the unpaid invoices would have to be recorded is December 31 at the end of the fiscal year. As has already been stated, all liabilities should be shown on the balance sheet at the end of the fiscal year and all purchases of merchandise and supplies should be shown in order to make a correct profit or loss statement. If this plan were followed by bookkeepers of small businesses, many hours of time could be saved.

Chapter XII

SPECIAL JOURNALS: THE CASH JOURNALS

THE ACCOUNTING DEFINITION OF cash is any medium of exchange that can be deposited in a bank at face value. Cash is the most liquid of all assets. Since an asset's liquidity is judged by the rapidity in which it turns to cash, no asset could be more liquid than cash itself. The principal sources of cash are cash sales of merchandise and cash collected from customers on their accounts.

Cash sales occur daily and collections from credit customers usually occur monthly. In designing the cash receipts journal, special columns should be reserved for these two principal sources of cash. A special journal for cash receipts should be designed so that all cash coming in from any source can be recorded in it.

The journal shown on page 54 is a typical cash receipts journal. It has special columns for the most frequent sources of cash. Cash coming in from any other source can be recorded in it because of the general column. The posting to the accounts receivable ledger should be completed daily and the names checked off as in the posting reference column beside the names of Henry Brown and John Jones. At the end of a month if the journal "proves," it should be posted. Cash is debited to account number 1 as indicated, Sales Discount to number 40, Accounts Receivable to number 23, Sales to number 27, the total of the general column is checked off so it will be posted to nowhere, Store Supplies is credited to number 31 and Purchases Returns and Allowances is credited to number 30.

CASH RECEIPTS JOURNAL

Date	Received from	Posting Reference	General Credit	Sales Credit	Accounts Receivable Credit	Sales Discount Debit	Cash Debit
19——							
July 2	Henry Brown	✓			$200	$4	$ 196
6	Purchases Returns & Allowances	30	$10				10
10	Sales	✓		$3,000			3,000
15	John Jones	31			100	2	98
30	Store Supplies		20				20
			$30 (V)	$3,000 (27)	$300 (23)	$6 (40)	$3,324 (1)

The credit to Purchases Returns and Allowances means that the owner purchased some merchandise from a supplier and paid cash for it, which indicates that he is not a regular supplier. When the merchandise was returned to him or an allowance was given due to damaged goods, he sent a check for $10. The credit to Store Supplies indicates that a neighboring merchant was out of bags, cartons, wrapping paper or some such item and some was sold to him at cost. The debit to Sales Discount indicates that cash discounts are given for prompt payment of accounts. The terms of the sale may have been 2/10/n/30, which means that if the account is paid within ten days after the sale the customer can discharge his obligation by paying only 98 percent. Sometimes terms such as this are used, 1/10/e.o.m., which means that the customer can deduct 1 percent if he pays within ten days after the end of the month.

It is a good business policy to pay promptly and receive discounts even if money has to be borrowed in order to do it. Two percent for ten days represents 72 percent for a year. Merchants can borrow at 6 percent, but few can make 72 percent—so taking discounts is about the best investment they can make.

Sales discount may be classified in several ways on the profit and loss statement. It may be considered a selling expense since prompt payment is closely related to selling. It may be classified as "other" expense or considered a minus income account and deducted from sales in the same manner as sales returns and allowances.

Most cash payments are charged to creditors and to operating expenses. In designing a cash payments journal for a business a study of the canceled checks should be made and special columns used for the most frequent expenses. If many cash purchases of merchandise were made, a special column for purchases should be used. Since most businesses buy on credit, a purchases column will be omitted, leaving one special column on the cash disbursements journal.

CASH PAYMENTS JOURNAL

Date	Check No.	Paid to	Posting Reference	General Debit	Accounts Payable Debit	Purchase Discount Credit	Cash Credit
19—							
July 5	3	Store Supplies	31	$ 50			$ 50
7	4	Acme Company	v		$100	$2	98
10	5	Prepaid Insurance	42	120			120
15	6	Ajax Corporation	v		200	4	196
30	7	John Doe, Drawing	2	200			200
30	8	Wages Expense	8	600			600
				$970	$300	$6	$1,264
				(v)	(3)	(44)	(1)

After learning to post from one multi-column journal, it is easy to post from another because the principle is the same. It must be remembered to post daily to subsidiary accounts receivable and accounts payable ledgers and to check them off as has been done in this journal. The journal should be proved before posting. One should be able to explain how this journal was posted at the end of the month. If any difficulty is encountered, reference should be made to the explanation of posting from the cash receipts journal. All that has to be done is to find the posting reference numbers. If they are in parenthesis at the bottom of a column, reference to the top of the column will indicate the name of the account. If they are in the posting reference column, a glance to the left of the number shows the name of the account.

Purchase discount needs little explanation because sales discount has been explained and a sales discount to one firm is a purchase discount to another firm. Sales discount and purchase discount are the same thing, depending on whether one is buying or selling. Purchase discount is classified as "other" income on the profit and loss statement or as a minus cost account in the cost of goods sold section, which reduces the cost of the goods purchased. The treasurer of the firm might insist that purchase discounts be reported as other income to show how much profit he was making for the firm by being alert. The purchasing agent may insist just as loudly that it should be shown as a deduction from the cost of the goods purchased so that it would indicate a shrewd purchasing technique.

Chapter XIII

POTPOURRI

Discounts Lost

IMPORTANT INFORMATION is withheld from the proprietor if purchase discounts are recorded in the traditional manner. He sees purchase discount on the profit and loss statement and feels pretty good about it, but he is left to wonder if all of them are being taken. He usually does not know whether 100 percent of them or 10 percent of them are being taken. He can remedy this by insisting that purchase discounts not be recorded at all. Instead of the usual recording of a $100 purchase, 2/10/n/30, he should insist that the purchase be recorded by debiting Purchases $98 and crediting Accounts Payable $98. If this account is paid within ten days, it can be paid by a check for $98. If the account is not paid within ten days, a check has to be written for $100. The extra $2 debit is charged to an account entitled "discounts lost," and it stands out like a neon light on the profit and loss statement among the general expenses. The proprietor knows exactly how much money office inefficiency is costing him under this system and he does not have to guess. Naturally an internal check such as this causes greater efficiency. The profit will be the same, for $100 cost and $2 income gives the same result as a $98 cost.

Partial Payments Discounts

Beginning accountants find some difficulty in determining the discount on partial payments. If a customer pays his entire bill of $400, they have no difficulty in recording it if he is to receive 2 percent discount. However if he sends a check for $200 within the discount period and the terms are 2 percent discount on any amount paid within the discount period, recording the transaction becomes an ordeal for many of them. How much discount should be given the man? The answer usually received is $4, but that is not enough. He would have been given a discount of $4 if he had paid $196. The answer is $204.08. The man is allowed to discharge his obligation by paying 98 percent ($200 ÷ .98 = $204.08). He wants credit for 100 percent. Whatever the discount—2 percent, 3 percent—the amount of 1 percent should be determined and the debtor given credit for 100 percent.

Cash Short or Over

The amount of cash that the cash register tape indicates should be in the register is seldom there. Anyone who has had experience with cash registers knows this. This difference almost always results from errors in making change. This cash short or over should be recorded in an account titled "cash short or over." Cash short is entered on the left side of the account and cash over is entered on the right. During the year the balance may be on either side. At the end of the year it would be one or the other. If it is short (debit balance), it is classified as general expense or "other" expense. If it is over (credit balance), it is classified as "other" income. If the sales as indicated by the tape should be $1,000 but only $990 are in the register, the sale should be recorded as $1,000 and an entry made in the cash payments journal debiting Cash Over or Short $10 and crediting Cash $10. If the reverse is true, $990 in sales should be recorded and $10 recorded in the cash receipts journal as a debit to Cash and a credit to Cash Short or Over. If one finds a $20 counterfeit bill in the cash drawer, what should he do?

Merchandise Inventory Adjustment

In a mercantile business the adjusting entry for merchandise inventory is a little different than the entry used in adjusting supplies. Purchases of merchandise are charged to the purchases account. Sales of merchandise are credited to the sales account. That means that the amount that was in the merchandise inventory account at the beginning of the fiscal period will be in the account when a trial balance is taken at the end of the fiscal period. Merchandise inventory is adjusted like this on the work sheet:

Account No.	Name of Account	Trial Balance		Adjustments		Profit & Loss		Balance Sheet	
		Debit	Credit	Debit	Credit	Debit	Credit	Debit	Credit
6	Merchandise Inventory	$6,000		$8,000	$6,000			$ 8,000	
	Profit & Loss Summary			6,000	8,000	$ 6,000	$ 8,000		
						30,000	40,000		
	Net Profit					10,000			$10,000
						$40,000	$40,000	$50,000	$50,000

At the end of the previous fiscal period the merchandise inventory was physically counted and found to be $6,000. At that time the account was adjusted and the balance of $6,000 left in it, and so it appears on the trial balance at $6,000. Purchases and sales of merchandise have been made and the period ends. Again the inventory is counted and this time is found to be $8,000. It is adjusted by crediting the inventory with $6,000 (which makes it nothing), and debiting it with the correct amount, $8,000. The opposite debit and credit is made to the profit and loss summary account. This is the same account used in making closing entries. Now why use four entries when one could have debited the inventory with $2,000 and credited Profit and Loss Summary with $2,000 and made it correct? Four entries are used in order to get the beginning merchandise inventory ($6,000) and the ending inventory ($8,000) into the profit and loss columns so that all the information needed for the preparation of a profit and loss statement will be there. This enables one to prepare the statement without looking elsewhere for needed information. This is just one of many ways to adjust merchandise inventory. This is one of the best ways because a principle is used which is used for a manufacturing enterprise as well as for a mercantile business. Actually, one can credit the old inventory, debit the new, and do the reverse to purchases, sales, and any income or expense account and the profit will be correct. Since these methods correct inventory but make something else incorrect at the same time, they are not recommended. The inventory can be adjusted by skipping the adjustment columns and writing the old inventory on the left of profit and loss, the new on the right of profit and loss and the new on the left of the balance sheet columns. The same figures are in the same columns but placed differently. The closing entries would correct the inventory.

Time may be saved and arithmetical computations eliminated altogether if the profit and loss summary account is closed into itself in making closing entries for a mercantile business. If this were to be done in the above illustration, the account, after posting the closing entries, would appear as follows:

Profit and Loss Summary	
$ 6,000	$ 8,000
8,000	6,000
30,000	40,000
10,000	

The debit of $6,000 and the credit of $8,000 are due to posting the adjusting entries. The debit of $8,000 is made because each account on the credit side of the profit and loss columns is debited. The $40,000 is the total of all the credits. The $6,000 credit is made because each account with a debit balance is credited. The $30,000 is the total of all the debit balances. The $10,000 debit is made to close the account. If every debit and every credit is closed, the balance of the profit and loss summary account will be the same amount that is already disclosed by the work sheet. This balance is closed into the proprietorship or the drawing account without having to determine its balance by arithmetic and risking a crucial error. Unless the amounts in the profit and loss summary account in the profit and loss columns on the work sheet are closed, as all the others, these amounts must be subtracted from the column totals or the expenses and incomes must be added again. This extra arithmetic and the chance of error should be avoided.

The income and cost of sales sections of a profit and loss statement for a merchandising business appear like this:

REED DRUG COMPANY

Profit and Loss Statement

For the year ending December 31, 19___

Income:		
Sales		$40,000
Less: Sales Returns & Allowances		2,000
Net Sales		38,000
Cost of Sales:		
Merchandise Inventory Jan. 1, 19—		$20,000
Purchases	$23,000	
Less: Purchases Returns & Allowances	1,000	
Net Purchases		22,000
Freight in		2,000
Goods Available for Sale		44,000
Less: Merchandise Inventory Dec. 31, 19—		16,000
Cost of Goods Sold:		28,000
Gross Profit on Sales		$10,000

The operating expenses are classified into selling and general. When these totals are subtracted from gross profit, it leaves net profit from operations. There may be "other" income to be added such as Purchase Discount or Interest Income, and there may be "other" expense to be deducted, such as Sales Discount and Interest Expense. When these are considered, the remainder is net profit.

The accuracy of the inventories is very important in determining profits or losses. After a year's transactions have been recorded, the higher the ending inventory the higher is the owner's profit. When a business is begun, the proprietor can choose his inventory method. Once he has chosen it however, he must stick to it (or get Washington's permission to change it). The Internal Revenue Service knows that as long as a firm uses the same inventory method the Government is going to get all that is coming to it in income taxes. If a mistake is made and the inventory is undervalued, resulting in a lower profit, just as sure as the sun rises, the next year's profit will be overstated by the same amount if the inventory is taken correctly the following year. The ending inventory of one year becomes the beginning inventory of the next year, so whatever an inventory error does to profit in one year it will do the opposite in the next year.

The most conservative method is cost or market, whichever is lower, because this leaves inventory at the lowest amount possible of all the accepted inventory methods. More people probably use actual cost to value inventories than any other method. Other methods are First-In, First-Out (Fifo), Last-In, First-Out (Lifo) and Average. Fifo applies the first costs to the first sales, which is logical. Lifo applies the last costs to the first sales which is illogical except for certain types of businesses. If a business is selling sand, gravel, coal, or iron from a pile, the last costs are actually the first sales.

Chapter   XIV

REVERSING ENTRIES

WITHOUT REVERSING entries, offices throughout the country would go through a very trying experience the first few weeks of every year. Reversing entries allow office workers, clerks, bookkeepers and accountants to record any transaction the same way every time it is recorded. Any accounting gimmick that will allow this is well worth learning. It is hoped that after this discussion reversing entries will be understood. If they are not, one thing is certain—anyone can know for sure "which" adjusting entries to reverse even if the "why" comes later.

The accountant can reduce the number of reversing

entries, but he cannot eliminate them altogether due to the accrued adjustments.

A rule is in order. If the adjusting entry for an accrued item or a deferred item sets up a new balance sheet account, the adjusting entry should be reversed. An accrued item is anything that accumulates, either receivable or payable. Rent, interest and wages are good examples. A deferred item is something paid or received in advance such as rent, insurance or interest. A new balance sheet account is one that is not on the trial balance. In making accrued or deferred adjustments on the work sheet, if the accountant has to write in the name of a balance sheet account then that entry should be reversed. There is a very good reason why this should be done. Imagine a young lady working for a firm that has many notes receivable, with people constantly coming in and paying the interest on the notes. She has been taught that she should debit Cash and credit Interest Income for the amount of the interest. She starts to work in April and learns her job well. At the end of December the accountant figures all the interest that has accrued on all the notes and records the adjusting entry. Our young lady comes to work on January 2 a little out of sorts. She begins to record the interest payments as they come in in the same manner she has for ten months. Suddenly the office manager informs her a bit brusquely that she cannot record the interest payments the way she is doing it! "I've been recording them this way for ten months," she replies, and adds a little sarcastically, "If I have been doing it wrong, why haven't you told me before now?" He tries to explain that it is because of the accrued interest that was recorded in December and that part of the payment must be credited to Interest Receivable and part to Interest Income; but by this time she is well on her way back to the employment agency, and no one could blame her.

Suppose this imaginary firm had had accrued interest receivable of $400 on December 31. The adjusting entry would have been a debit to Interest Receivable and a credit to Interest Income. The closing entry would have closed Interest Income. If the accountant stops here, he is asking for loads of trouble because any time a person makes a payment, the accountant would have to analyze the amount and see how many days' interest was owed on December 31 and credit Interest Receivable for that amount and credit Interest Income for the remainder. He could forestall all this nonsense by making an entry exactly the reverse of the adjusting entry. This would leave Interest Income open with a debit balance. Had this been done the young lady could have recorded the same way she had become accustomed to and they would not have had to train a new employee. Reversing entries are sometimes called "readjusting" entries.

Imagine a small firm with twenty employees. A clerk has been taught to record in a cash payments journal with a debit column for Wages Expense and credit columns for old age benefits payments, withholding taxes, a few other deductions and cash. Pay days rarely come on December 31 and most of the time an adjustment for wages payable would have to be made. Pity the poor clerk when he is told that for the first pay day in January Wages Payable will have to be charged with two days' pay and Wages Expense with three days' pay. What a dilemma! The best way to solve the dilemma is not to be in it. Office managers avoid such situations as this by using reversing entries, as they enable them to record transactions the same way every time they occur, regardless of the date.

Reversing entries for deferred items can be eliminated altogether by making original entries in balance sheet accounts. For instance, if insurance is paid in advance, it should be charged to Prepaid Insurance. If rent is received in advance, it should be credited to Unearned Rental Income or Prepaid Rental Income. When these accounts are adjusted, an expense or income account is set up and no reversing entry is needed. If anyone is ever in doubt about which adjusting entries to reverse, he should place a ruler across the work sheet at the trial balance total. He should look below the ruler in the balance sheet columns. If he finds any figures in these columns, the adjusting entry that set them up should be reversed. (At the end of the first year of operations merchandise inventory would be there but should not be reversed. It would not be there after one year. For this reason the rule stated that all adjustments of accrued and deferred items that set up new balance sheet accounts should be reversed.)

Reversing entries for accrued items have great value as has been illustrated. Reversing entries for deferred items have little value. They are easy to learn and should be learned as auditors would rather make them than explain them. In auditing a client's records where the client has recorded rent paid in advance as Rent Expense, an adjusting entry would cause a new balance sheet account, Prepaid Rent, to be opened. This should be reversed, but the only plausible reason is that the client had the rent expense account open in his ledger and it is assumed that he wanted it there, so a reversing entry allows the account to remain open.

To prove the value of reversing entries one should record an adjusting entry, such as a debit to Interest Expense and a credit to Interest Payable, in "T" accounts. He should close the interest expense account. He should make the reversing entry. He should record the payment of $10 interest. Because he has made the reversing entry he can record by debiting Interest Expense $10 and crediting Cash $10. If he has not made the reversing entry he cannot record at all because he does not know how much of the $10 was accrued on December 31. He could look it up or compute the interest after being given the number of days accrued and the interest rate. This will at least prove that reversing entries save analyzing time. In adjusting a trial balance if the words receivable, payable, deferred, unearned, or prepaid have to be added, the adjusting entry should be reversed. Reversing entries are dated the first day of the succeeding fiscal period and are labeled plainly.

Date	Description	Posting Reference	Debit	Credit
19__	*Reversing Entries*			
Jan. 1	Interest Payable		$10	
	Interest Expense			$10

Chapter XV

ACCRUED AND DEFERRED ITEMS

SINCE ACCRUE means to accumulate, this type of adjustment cannot be avoided at the end of a fiscal year. Income accrues to business firms such as interest on notes receivable, and many expenses accrue, such as interest, wages and taxes. There are only two ways to adjust accrued items. If the accrued item is receivable, income has to be credited. If the accrued item is payable, expense has to be debited.

Receivable—Income
Expense—Payable

All accrued adjustments can be made by substituting a descriptive word. For instance, if $10 interest on a note is receivable, the adjusting entry is to debit Interest Receivable $10, and credit Interest Income $10. To the person or business that owed the $10 the adjusting entry would be to debit Interest Expense and credit Interest Payable. There are no other ways to make these adjustments. If rent, taxes, insurance or anything else has accrued, one merely substitutes one of these words for interest.

Adjusting deferred, prepaid or unearned items cannot be this simple because of the original recording. As long as different people record transactions they will record them differently. Rent paid in advance by one firm may be recorded by a debit to Prepaid Rent, while down the street the same transaction may be recorded as a debit to Rent Expense. One of the firms receiving the money may record it as a debit to Cash and a credit to Rent Income, while the other firm receiving the money may record the transaction as a debit to Cash and a credit to Unearned Rent Income. The words unearned, prepaid and deferred have the same meaning in this situation. Assume $3,600 was paid for three years' rent and adjustments are made after one year has elapsed. There would be two choices in recording payment of the money and two choices in recording receipt as follows:

Payment		Receipt	
Prepaid Rent	Rent Expense	Prepaid Rent Income	Rent Income
$3,600 or	$3,600	$3,600 or	$3,600

After one year has passed there is $1,200 Rent Expense and Rent Income, and $2,400 Prepaid Rent and Prepaid Rent Income. If Prepaid Rent is to be adjusted, it must be credited $1,200 and Rent Expense must be debited $1,200. If Rent Expense is to be adjusted, it must be credited $2,400 and Prepaid Rent debited $2,400. On the other side of the fence, if Rent Income is to be adjusted, it must be debited with $2,400 and Prepaid, Unearned, or Deferred Rent Income must be credited with $2,400. If Prepaid Rent Income is to be adjusted, it must be debited with $1,200 and Rent Income must be credited with $1,200.

Prospective accountants should reason out these adjustments and not depend on memory. Here is a device that may help.

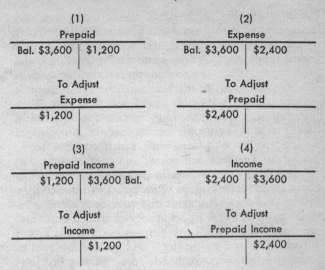

All other deferred items are adjusted in the same manner. Only the names are different. All accrued adjustments set up new balance sheet accounts and should be reversed. Some deferred adjustments, such as the second and fourth above, set up new balance sheet accounts and should be reversed.

Chapter XVI

INTEREST AND DISCOUNTING NOTES

INTEREST IS THE PRICE paid for credit or money paid for the use of money. Business runs on credit and if all credit were suddenly cut off, the economy of the country would all but grind to a screeching halt.

Credit is fine but, as in other things, individuals and business firms should use it with moderation. Consumers should understand interest and how to figure it. Few people really do, including some college graduates and professors. Advertisements in professional magazines offer to lend money to teachers and others at 36 percent per year. The ads do not say 36 percent a year. They just state that the agreed rate of interest is 3 percent a month; that many people use this service is evidenced by the number of advertisements that continue to be published. Teachers and others join credit unions that charge higher rates of interest than the local bank. The same credit unions quite often pay less interest than savings and loan companies that have each account insured up to $20,000 by an agency of the Federal Government. When goods are purchased on credit and 6 percent is added to the total and divided by twelve, twenty-four or thirty-six months, only the very first payment is at the 6 percent rate, with each additional payment the rate gets higher and higher. Even banks charge a little more than 6 percent when the interest is paid in advance on a loan. (Interest rates are changing often.)

The 60-day 6 percent method of computing interest is a handy device. The interest on $6,197.53 at 6 percent for 6,000 days is $6,197.53. For 600 days the decimal point should be moved one place to the left and the answer is $619.75. For 60 days the decimal is moved another place to the left and the answer is $61.98. For 6 days the decimal is moved one more place to the left and the answer is $6.20. The decimal may be moved to the right also, but 60,000 days is a mighty long time. Usually it is quicker to use this method. If any combination of percentages multiplied by the number of days equals 360, two places are pointed off. Six percent times 60 days equals 360; 5 percent times 72 days equals 360; 9 percent times 40 days equals 360, and so on. If the percentage multiplied by the days equals 36, three places are pointed off. If the percentage times the days equals 360, two places are pointed off. If the percentage times the days equals 3,600, one place is pointed off and so on. Being able to ascertain the interest for 60 days makes it easy to determine the interest for 45 days, 20 days, or some fraction of 60. Knowing the interest for 6 days, it becomes easy to obtain the interest for 18 days, 2 days, or some multiple or fraction of 6. The interest on $619.82 at 6 percent for 38 days is relatively easy to determine by the 60-day, 6 percent method.

$3.10	30 days
.62	6 days
.21	2 days
$3.93	38 days

Notes are interest-bearing and non-interest-bearing. Bankers prefer non-interest-bearing notes because their use enables the banks to deduct the interest in advance, which enables them to make a little more profit on the money they lend. To borrow $200 from a bank for 60 days at 6 percent, the borrower would have to sign a note for $200 to obtain $198 in cash. At 6 percent the borrower should have the use of $200 for 60 days for a charge of $2. If he receives less than $200, the rate is a little higher. If one considers all the loans that banks make, this extra income to them becomes more than trivial. The entry to record the previous transaction is:

Cash	$198	
Interest Expense	2	
Notes Payable		$200

Cash should be checked to avoid posting and the $198 recorded in the cash receipts journal. Cash should be debited in the cash column and Notes Payable credited in the general column. Notes Payable should be checked in the general column to avoid double posting. Accepting less than the face value or the maturity value of a note is termed "discounting" a note. The maturity value of a note is the face (amount written on the note) if the note is non-interest-bearing. If the note bears interest, the maturity value is the face plus the interest.

A customer's non-interest-bearing note for $200 discounted 60 days before it is due is recorded in this manner:

Cash	$198	
Interest Expense	2	
Notes Receivable—J. Jones		$200

Cash should be checked and $198 recorded in the cash receipts journal as a debit to Cash and a credit to Notes Receivable with Notes Receivable being checked to avoid double posting. If the above note had been a one-year, 5 percent interest-bearing-note, discounted 60 days before it was due, the problem becomes a little more involved because the arithmetic becomes more difficult. With a little math, this formula becomes very handy.

Maturity value (face + interest)		$210
Discount Rate	6 percent	
Discount Period	60 days	2.10
Proceeds		$207.90

The maturity value of a $200, 5 percent one-year note is $210. To discount this amount for 60 days at 6 percent the decimal is moved to the left two places and subtracted to get the proceeds. To record:

Cash	$207.90	
Interest Income		$ 7.90
Notes Receivable—J. Jones		$200.00

Since this entry has a debit to Cash and a credit to Interest Income and Notes Receivable, it may be recorded in the cash receipts journal with no recording in the general journal. If it is recorded in the general journal, Cash should be checked as usual and Notes Receivable should be checked in the cash receipts journal to avoid double posting.

Discounting a note in this manner makes the endorser of the note liable if the signer of the note does not pay it. Since the endorser may have to pay it, a contingent (possible) liability of $200 should be shown as a footnote on any balance sheet that is prepared before the maturity date. To avoid the footnote a contingent liability, Notes Receivable Discounted, may be credited instead of Notes Receivable. This account is subtracted from Notes Receivable on the balance sheet to show the notes on hand.

When a note is not paid by the maker at maturity, the note is said to be dishonored. If the above note had not been paid by the maker (J. Jones), the endorser would have to pay it. Banks charge a collection fee for this service, so the endorser would have to pay $200 (face) plus $10 (interest) plus $5 collection fee. The endorser should credit Cash for the total amount, $215, and the entire amount should be charged to Accounts Receivable —J. Jones. This entry is made in the cash payments journal whether a check is written or whether the bank simply charges the endorser's account with $215. No attempt should be made to separate the charges into different accounts such as interest and collection fees. The maker of the note owes the endorser $215, so this amount should be charged to him. The endorser will make an effort to collect it all, but he may not receive any of it. The recording of bad debts will be discussed in the next chapter.

Sometimes a customer will reduce his debt by giving an interest-bearing note which he has received from one of his own customers. When this is the case he should be given credit for the face of the note and the accrued interest. The receipt of a six-month, 6 percent note after one month has gone by would be recorded in this manner:

Notes Receivable	$200	
Interest Income	1	
Accounts Receivable—J. Jones		$201

This is an example of using the reversing principle in making an original entry. By recording the month's interest of $1 as a debit to Interest Income, the same account can be credited with the six months' interest of $6 when it is received. This will leave the $5 which has actually been earned.

Interest Expense is classified as "other" expense and Interest Income is classified as "other" income on the profit and loss statement.

Chapter   XVII

BAD DEBTS

AMOUNTS REQUIRED for adjustments of inventories, accrued and deferred items can be computed by counting or by the use of mathematical processes. In adjusting the loss from bad debts an estimate has to be used. This amount is computed, but it is only an intelligent guess.

If accounts receivable are reported on a balance sheet at the total amount, this asset is likely to be overvalued. If many sales are made on credit, some of the customers will not pay, regardless of how carefully they are screened originally. In order not to place too high a value on accounts receivable, an attempt is made to reduce it to a more realistic figure by an adjusting entry. Past experience or the experience of others in the same type of business may indicate that 3 percent of accounts receivable at the end of any given year probably will not be collected. A different estimate may be made by different firms. Some may use a smaller percentage of the total sales. If a firm has $10,000 on account and it is estimated that 4 percent will not be collected, the adjusting entry will be:

Bad Debts Expense	$400	
Allowance for Bad Debts		$400

Bad Debts Expense is classified as a selling or a general expense on the profit and loss statement. Allowance for bad debts is classified as a minus asset account and is deducted from Accounts Receivable on the balance sheet.

Current Assets		
Accounts Receivable	$10,000	
Less: Allowance for Bad Debts	400	$9,600

If a firm has notes receivable as well as accounts receivable, the two accounts are added together and the allowance is subtracted from the total.

Showing the accounts receivable at a value of $9,600 on the balance sheet does not mean that now the accounts receivable account is exactly correct. It only means that, in the opinion of the maker of the statement, it is more nearly correct than the total amount of $10,-000. Since Internal Revenue allows this estimate to be made in advance for tax purposes, most accountants use it. This is "the bird in the hand is worth two in the bush" theory of accounting.

When the allowance has been set up, the account should be used when a bad account is to be written off. If Bill Smith's account becomes bad, the entry is:

Allowance for Bad Debts	$30	
Accounts Receivable—Bill Smith		$30

A less complicated way of handling bad debts is to use

the direct write-off method. In this method no allowance is set up. When the account becomes bad, as in the above illustration, an account "bad debts expense" would be charged and Accounts Receivable—Bill Smith credited.

Sometimes an account that has previously been written off is collected. The proper recording of a bad debt collected depends on the manner in which it was written off. Bad debts taken as a deduction (as in the direct write-off method) but subsequently recovered, must be included in gross income for the year received according to Internal Revenue. It is recorded in this manner whenever it is received:

```
Cash                              $30
  Bad Debts Collected                    $30
  (Collected the account of
  Bill Smith previously written off)
```

Bad Debts Collected would be classified as "other" income on the profit and loss statement.

If the reserve (allowance) method is used, the recoveries of bad debts are not included in gross income. Instead, the taxpayer credits the reserve with the amount of the bad debt collections. If Bill Smith's account had been written off by a debit to Allowance for Bad Debts and subsequently recovered, the entry would be:

```
Cash                              $30
  Allowance for Bad Debts                $30
  (Collected the account of Bill
  Smith previously written off)
```

In either of the above cases a notation should be made in Bill Smith's account in the accounts receivable ledger stating that he had settled the account. This may affect credit policy toward him in the future. Bill Smith's account may be reopened and then closed in this manner; if it is desired.

Accounts Receivable—Bill Smith	$30	
Allowance for Bad Debts		$30
Cash	$30	
Accounts Receivable—Bill Smith		$30

An effective method in determining the proper amount to include in the allowance for bad debts account is the "aging" process. The accounts are classified as, 30 days past due, 60 days past due, 90 days past due, etc. This method is not quite as good as one a merchant used in 1829. This merchant had $35,000 on account. Each debtor's name was listed and the amount he owed was entered in one of three columns headed, "Desperate," "Doubtful," and "Ought to be Good!" This was before anyone in the world had ever dreamed of a tax on income, but the merchant knew that all accounts were not good. This effective device gave him much information about them. He expected to collect all of the last column. He expected to collect a good part of the second column. Any collections from the first column he probably considered "gravy."

Chapter XVIII

DEPRECIATION

THE FINAL RESTING place for all machinery and other fixed assets, with the exception of land, is the junk yard. Paint, oil and repairs may prolong their lives, but sooner or later they must succumb to the inevitable. This decline in the value of assets due to wear and tear by use, or by decay caused by the elements of nature, is known as depreciation. Internal Revenue recognizes that depreciation is one of the most important costs of a business.

A debit to a fixed asset is a capital charge. A debit to an expense account is a revenue charge. The difference in them is a matter of time. With the exception of charges to land, all capital charges eventually become revenue charges.

The most common method of determining amounts to be charged to depreciation is the straight-line method. It is cost minus scrap value divided by the number of years of life. If a delivery truck is purchased at $4,200 and the estimated life is four years and the scrap value is $200, the amount to be charged to depreciation each year is $1,000. Cost ($4,200) minus scrap ($200) divided by the number of years life (4). The adjusting entry is:

Depreciation Expense	$1,000	
Allowance for Depreciation of Delivery Equipment		$1,000

The depreciation expense is a general expense and the allowance for depreciation of delivery equipment is a minus asset account. It is shown on the balance sheet in this manner:

Fixed Assets:		
Delivery Equipment	$4,200	
Less: Allowance for Depreciation	1,000	$3,200

To show the original cost and the present value of an asset is more desirable than to show the present value alone. For this reason the allowance account is credited in making the adjustment instead of the delivery equipment account itself.

If the delivery truck was sold for $3,400, it would be recorded in this manner:

Cash	$3,400	
Allowance for Depreciation	1,000	
Delivery Equipment		$4,200
Gain on Sale of Delivery Equipment		200

If the delivery equipment was exchanged for another of the same general type (list price $5,000) and $4,500 was allowed for the old equipment, the exchange would be recorded in this manner:

Delivery Equipment	$3,700	
Allowance for Depreciation	1,000	
Delivery Equipment		$4,200
Cash		500

Internal Revenue says that in the exchange of one fixed asset for another of the same general type no gain or loss may be recorded on the transaction for income tax purposes. The delivery equipment could be recorded at list price, $5,000, which would necessitate the recording of a gain of $1,300. Schedule "C" of the income tax return would have to differ from the regular profit and loss statement in this instance. Internal Revenue allows depreciation equal to the cost of a fixed asset. In this case one delivery truck valued at $3,200 and $500 cash were paid for the new asset, so $3,700 in depreciation charges will be allowed (minus scrap). Depreciation of the list price of $5,000 will not be allowed. To record the new truck at $5,000 is in harmony with accounting theory, but it adds confusion. When accounting theory and the Internal Revenue Code of 1954 are in direct contradiction, the accountant has to choose between the theoretical and the practical. In this instance, each side has staunch supporters.

When a fixed asset is traded during a fiscal period, the depreciation for that portion of a year must first be recorded. In the previous illustration if three months of a year had gone by before the trade, it would be recorded in this manner:

Depreciation Expense	$ 250	
Delivery Equipment	3,450	
Allowance for Depreciation	1,000	
Cash		$ 500
Delivery Equipment		4,200

In recording the depreciation for the fraction of a year, there is no need to credit Allowance for Depreciation, for this account has to be closed anyway. It is very easy to record the exchange of a fixed asset for another if everything already known is first recorded. Depreciation of $250 for three months is easy to determine. The old equipment is gone, so it is credited with its cost to make it nothing. The allowance that goes with the old equipment is closed. The cash paid out is credited. The difference between these debits and credits will always be the correct amount to be charged to the new asset. When all the known facts are recorded, the one unknown fact, the price of the new asset, comes up automatically.

The declining-balance method of computing depreciation was authorized by the Internal Revenue Code of 1954. This method allows twice the straight-line method of write-off without regard to salvage value. In the illustration used previously, cost was $4,200, scrap was $200 and the number of years life was four. On the straight-line method the depreciation percentage is 25 percent per year. On the declining-balance method the percentage would be 50 percent on the balance of the account.

Delivery Equipment	Allowance for Depreciation	
$4,200	$2,100	1st Year
	1,050	2nd Year
	525	3rd Year
	262.50	4th Year
	$3,937.50	

At the end of the fourth year the equipment would have a book value of $262.50. If it remains in use, one-half of its remaining balance would be charged to depreciation each year. An asset has to be depreciated for at least three years if this method is to be used.

The sum of the years-digits method is another accelerated depreciation method which was authorized by the 1954 Code. If this method were used in the previous example, the number of years life would be added, i.e., $4 + 3 + 2 + 1 = 10$. Cost ($4,200) minus scrap ($200) leaves $4,000 to be depreciated over four years. The first year's depreciation would be $4/10 \times \$4,000$. The next year's depreciation would be $3/10 \times \$4,000$, then 2/10, and then 1/10. This method has been referred to as the "reducing fraction" method, which describes it more adequately. Greater write-offs in the first years of an asset's life would tend to equalize the total cost over its life because repairs are greater toward the end.

First Year	Second Year	Third Year	Fourth Year
Repairs	Repairs	Repairs	Repairs
Depreciation	Depreciation	Depreciation	Depreciation

Other less commonly used depreciation methods are the working hours and the unit output methods. If a new machine is estimated to operate for 60,000 hours and during a fiscal year it operates 10,000 hours, the depreciation charge would be determined in this manner: Cost ($4,200) minus scrap ($200) times 1/6. If the machine was estimated to produce 60,000 units and during a fiscal year it produced 10,000 units, the depreciation charge would be determined in the same manner.

The depletion allowance for natural resources is determined in the same way. If it is estimated that a mineral deposit contains 60,000 tons of ore and 10,000 tons were excavated in one fiscal year, 1/6 of the cost of the mineral rights would be charged to depletion expense and an allowance for depletion would be credited. The latter is a minus asset and is subtracted from the asset (Mineral Rights) on the balance sheet.

Bulletin "F," Internal Revenue Service Publications Number 173, entitled "Tables of Useful Lives on Depreciable Property, is available as a guide to taxpayers and can be obtained from the Treasury Department for about thirty cents. It gives suggested, but not mandatory, lengths of life for most of the depreciable assets of the major industries.

Chapter XIX

PETTY CASH

IT IS GOOD BUSINESS policy to deposit all cash received in a bank and to make all cash payments by check. This results in a double record of cash, the business firm's record and the bank's record. Most banks do not charge for this service and many businesses avail themselves of this free bookkeeping. When this practice is followed, a small amount of cash, called petty cash, is kept on hand.

Some firms use petty cash books or analysis sheets to record the petty expenditures. These aid the accountant in determining the general journal entry to be used in recording the check written to replenish the fund.

A petty cash fund may be "imprest" or it may be fluctuating. If the imprest system of keeping petty cash is used, the petty cash balance remains intact. A check is written and cashed. This amount is charged to Petty Cash and Cash is credited. As amounts are withdrawn from the fund, receipts are kept. When the fund needs replenishing, a check is drawn for whatever amount has been used. This check is charged to Supplies, General Expenses, or whatever account properly describes the expenditures, and Cash is credited. The amount of the

PETTY CASH BOOK

Date	Explanation	Receipts	Payments	Office Supplies	General Expenses	Sundry Accounts	
							Store Supplies
May 1	Check No. 11	$50.00					
5			$ 3.00	$ 3.00			
8			5.00		$ 5.00		
10			5.00			$5.00	
15			5.00	5.00	5.00		
20			5.00		15.00		
25			15.00				
27			2.00	2.00			
27			5.00		5.00		
27	Totals	50.00	45.00	$10.00	$30.00	$5.00	
27	Balance		5.00				
		$50.00	$50.00				
27	Balance	5.00					
27	Check No. 50	45.00					

original check remains in the petty cash fund until the fund is increased or decreased due to the management policy.

If the fluctuating fund method is used, a check is written and cashed. This amount is charged to Petty Cash and credited to Cash. When the fund is to be replenished, accounts describing the expenditures are charged and Petty Cash is credited. When the replenishing check is written and cashed, Petty Cash is charged and Cash is credited.

Imprest Fund			Fluctuating Fund		
Petty Cash	$50		Petty Cash	$50	
Cash		$50	Cash		$50
(To establish)			(To establish)		
Office Supplies	10		Office Supplies	10	
Store Supplies	5		Store Supplies	5	
General Expenses	30		General Expenses	30	
Cash		45	Petty Cash		45
(To replenish)			(To record expenditures)		
			Petty Cash	45	
			Cash		45
			(To replenish)		

When an accounting system is designed for most small businesses, a combined cash journal usually replaces the various special journals. If only one person records, this is more satisfactory. The accounts that are used the most determine the column headings. A general debit and a general credit column are always used so that any transaction can be recorded in the combined cash journal. An illustration of a combined cash journal with posting references follows. Posting from all multi-columned journals is essentially the same. As in all journals of this type, it should be "proved" before posting. This one proves at $5,720.

COMBINED CASH JOURNAL

Date	Check No.	Explanation	Post. Ref.	General Dr.	General Cr.	Cash Dr.	Cash Cr.	Acct. Rec. Dr.	Acct. Rec. Cr.	Acct. Pay. Dr.	Acct. Pay. Cr.	Pur. Dr.	Sales Cr.	Sales Disc. Dr.	Pur. Disc. Cr.	Store Sup. Dr.
June 3	1	Rent Expense	27	200			200									
5		John Smith	✓					400					400			
7		Acme Co.	✓								600	600				
10		Fred Jones	✓					700					700			
12		Store Supply Co.	✓								100					100
13		John Smith	✓			392			400					8		
16	2	Acme Co.	✓				588			600					12	
17	3	Arch Corp.	✓				200									200
18		Fred Jones	✓			686			700					14		
20	4	Store Supply Co.	✓				98			100					2	
23		Basic Corp.	✓								900	900				
30	5	Wages Expense	29	800			800									
30		Interest Income	31		20	20										
				1,000	20	1,098	1,886	1,100	1,100	700	1,600	1,500	1,100	22	14	300
				(V)	(V)	(1)	(1)	(2)	(2)	(41)	(41)	(16)	(21)	(23)	(18)	(25)

GENERAL LEDGER

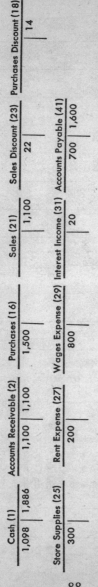

Cash (1)

1,098	1,886

Accounts Receivable (2)

1,100	1,100

Sales (21)

	1,100

Sales Discount (23)

22	

Purchases Discount (18)

	14

Store Supplies (25)

300	

Rent Expense (27)

200	

Purchases (16)

1,500	

Wages Expense (29)

800	

Interest Income (31)

	20

Accounts Payable (41)

700	1,600

ACCOUNTS RECEIVABLE LEDGER

Fred Jones

700	700

John Smith

400	400

ACCOUNTS PAYABLE LEDGER

Acme Co.

600	600

Basic Corp.

	900

Store Supply Co.

100	100

Chapter XX

CORRECTING ENTRIES

TIME HEALS many wounds and in accounting time corrects many mistakes. Errors in counting merchandise inventory, errors in adjusting accrued items, and errors in adjusting deferred items are all corrected by the passage of time. These errors make two fiscal periods incorrect by the same amounts and in opposite ways but, barring further errors, the next fiscal period will be correct. Errors in recording depreciation and bad debts will not correct themselves automatically.

When errors are discovered they should be corrected by one of several ways. If the wrong amount is recorded in a journal and it is discovered before the journal is posted, it may be corrected by drawing a neat line through the incorrect amount and writing in the correct amount. If an incorrect amount is posted to a ledger from a journal, a neat line may be drawn through the incorrect amount in the ledger account and the correct amount written in.

Most errors have to be corrected by a general journal entry. If Office Equipment is charged with $50 instead of Office Supplies, an entry debiting Office Supplies and crediting Office Equipment must be made. If J. Y. Browne's account in the accounts receivable ledger had been charged with $10 instead of J. V. Brown's account, an entry debiting one and crediting the other must be made. No entry is needed in the controlling account.

In taking a physical inventory of merchandise on December 31, $20 of merchandise was overlooked, and the adjusting entry was recorded. If this error is discovered before the closing entries have been made, Merchandise Inventory should be debited and Profit and Loss Summary should be credited. If this error is discovered after the closing entries have been made, the inventory should be debited and Proprietorship should be credited.

In a succeeding fiscal period it is discovered that a purchase of merchandise on credit from the Able Company had been made in the preceding fiscal period but had not been recorded. A liability had been omitted from the balance sheet and the omission of a purchase caused the profit to be too great. Debit Proprietorship and credit Accounts Payable—Able Company to correct.

In a succeeding fiscal period it is discovered that a sale of merchandise on credit to Fred Dark had not been recorded. Debit Accounts Receivable—Fred Dark and credit Proprietorship to correct.

The reversing principle should be used in making some correcting entries. If Interest Receivable of $10 was not recorded during the previous fiscal period, the correcting entry would be to debit Interest Income and credit Proprietorship with $10. Why debit Interest Income? Because correcting entries should be made to reflect the balances that would have been in the ledger if no error had been made. If no error had been made, the adjusting entry would have been a debit to Interest Receivable and a credit to Interest Income. The closing entry would have closed Interest Income. The reversing entry would have opened Interest Income by a debit. If no error had been made, the $10 debit would be in Interest Income and profit would have been $10 more, which would have increased Proprietorship by $10.

If accrued wages payable of $100 had been omitted during the previous fiscal period, the correcting entry would be to debit Proprietorship and to credit Wages Expense. If no error had been made, Proprietorship would have been $100 less because of the expense and Wages Expense would have had a credit balance due to the reversing entry.

An error in arithmetic was made and depreciation of store equipment was understated by $200 in a previous fiscal period. When detected in the succeeding fiscal period Proprietorship should be debited and Allowance for Depreciation of Store Equipment should be credited.

A merchandise purchase of $40 was charged to Sales Returns and Allowances. The error went unnoticed until January of the following fiscal year. When discovered, no correcting entry was made because Sales Returns and Allowances and Purchases have the same effect on profits and, since both of these had been closed, no correcting entry could be made.

In making extensions on merchandise inventory sheets an error in arithmetic was made and the amount was overstated by $300. This would make profits $300 more for the current year and, if not corrected, the profits would be $300 less in the succeeding year. In the current year the cost of goods sold is understated, making more profit. Since the ending inventory of one year becomes the beginning inventory of the next, the cost of goods sold in the next is overstated, making profits $300 too little in that year. Internal Revenue prefers that errors be corrected when located and amended income tax returns be made. To correct the above error, rather than waiting for time to correct it, Merchandise Inventory would be credited with $300 and Proprietorship debited with $300.

In adjusting Rent Expense, Prepaid Rent was charged with $400 and Rent Expense was credited with $400. The amount of the debit and credit should have been $300. In a succeeding fiscal period the correcting entry would be a debit to Proprietorship and a credit to Rent Expense. The $100 extra charge to the asset Prepaid Rent made $100 too much profit for the period, so Proprietorship must be decreased by a debit. The $100 credit is made to Rent Expense instead of Prepaid Rent because the reversing entry would have closed Prepaid Rent and left Rent Expense with a credit balance had no error been made. This type of reversing entry has very little value. It must be assumed that, since the rent was originally charged to the expense account, whoever recorded the original entry must have had a reason satisfactory to himself for recording the transaction in that manner. As was mentioned in the chapter on reversing entries, all reversing entries except the accrued adjustments can be eliminated if real accounts are used in making original entries instead of nominal accounts.

A credit sale to Ted Reed of $100 was not recorded in the fiscal year the sale was made. In the following year Mr. Reed paid his account and the transaction was recorded as a debit to Cash, $100, and a credit to Sales, $100. The correcting entry would be a debit to Sales and a credit to Proprietorship because it was not a sale in the year in which it was recorded and if it had been recorded as a sale in the previous year, the profit would have been $100 more, resulting in $100 more net worth.

A credit purchase was not recorded in December of the year in which the purchase was made although the merchandise was included in the ending inventory. When discovered in the succeeding fiscal period the correcting entry would be to debit Proprietorship and to credit Accounts Payable. If the purchase had been recorded properly, the cost of sales would have been more and the profit would have been less and the liability would have been in the ledger.

If, in the previous example, the same error was made except that the merchandise was not included in the merchandise inventory, the correcting entry would be to debit Merchandise Inventory and to credit Accounts Payable. Failing to record a purchase and omitting the purchase from the ending inventory does not affect profits because purchases are added to beginning inventory and ending inventory is subtracted to obtain the cost of sales. Omitting any amount from a figure that is added and also omitting the same amount from a figure that is subtracted could not change the cost of sales or the profit.

During a fiscal period a bookkeeper charged a sales return to the purchases account. When discovered in the next fiscal period no correcting entry could be made because both of these accounts have the same effect on profits. Sales returns reduce income and purchases of merchandise increase cost of sales, so it is six of one and a half dozen of the other.

A purchase return that was credited to the sales account would not require a correcting entry in a succeeding fiscal period for the same reason.

When correcting entries have to be made in a succeeding fiscal period, the effect of the error on profits should first be determined. This will give the clue to decrease or increase Proprietorship. Next it should be determined if the reversing principle should be used in making the correcting entry.

Chapter XXI

THE VOUCHER SYSTEM

THE VOUCHER SYSTEM is a method of internal control that requires a written authorization for each expenditure. In double entry accounting there are many systems. Several of them have been discussed. Keeping accounts receivable in a subsidiary ledger controlled by an account in the general ledger is one system. Any controlling account that controls a ledger is a system. Two systems of keeping petty cash have been discussed. The voucher system is a method of recording payments, nothing else.

Voucher is a term that applies to all business papers in general accounting. In this chapter it applies to a business paper that is prepared when payments are to be made. The vouchers may be any size, shape or color. The accounts most often debited for expenditures may be printed on the voucher with blank lines to be used for the unusual expenditures.

After vouchers have been approved for payment they are recorded in a journal with columns for accounts payable, purchases and supplies and a general column for unusual expenditures. This journal is called a voucher register. In this system the cash payments journal is called a check register and each check pays a specific voucher. As each voucher is paid, the date and the check number may be recorded in a special column on the voucher register.

No accounts payable ledger is kept if the voucher system is used. The unpaid vouchers are kept in a file. This is one record of the creditors. All unpaid vouchers can be determined from the register by checking the paid column. To keep a third record of accounts payable would be too much of a good thing, so the ledger is usually omitted.

The voucher system is easily understood when it is realized that all expenditures are first recorded as if they were accrued, then paid. In general accounting there is a debit to Wages Expense and a credit to Cash when wages are paid. In the voucher system there is a debit to Wages Expense and a credit to Accounts Payable which is recorded in the voucher register, and a debit to Accounts Payable and a credit to Cash which is recorded in the check register. There is an extra debit and a credit to Accounts Payable for all cash purchases. In general accounting a cash purchase of merchandise is recorded as a debit to Purchases and a credit to Cash. In the voucher system the same transaction is recorded using these two accounts but also a debit and a credit to Accounts Payable.

General Accounting			Voucher System		
Purchases	Cash	Purchases	Accounts Payable		Cash
$100	$100	$100	$100	$100	$100

The term "vouchers payable" is used in many voucher systems instead of "accounts payable." The terms are synonymous.

The red tape involved in using the voucher system causes additional expenses. A proprietor has to make a decision as to whether or not the control of expenditures in this manner is worth the additional expense.

The rigidity of the voucher register makes corrections a bit awkward. If an error is made in recording a voucher before the register is posted, a line may be drawn through the entire transaction—the old voucher canceled and a new one prepared and recorded. If a purchase return or allowance is received before the register is posted, the amount of the allowance may be written above the amount in the purchase and accounts payable columns and circled. An amount in a column that has been circled or written in a different color means the opposite of the column heading of debit or credit.

Possibly the most difficult thing to remember about the voucher system is how to record a purchase return after the register has been posted. Suppose a credit purchase of $500 has been recorded in the register and posted as a debit to Purchases and a credit to Accounts Payable. Then an allowance of $50 is received. A general journal entry is recorded.

Accounts Payable	$500	
Purchases		$450
Purchases Returns and Allowance		50

The old voucher is now canceled and a new voucher for

$450 is prepared and recorded in the register as a debit to Purchases and a credit to Accounts Payable. When these entries are posted the following results:

Purchases		Accounts Payable		Purchases Returns & Allowance
$500	$450	$500	$500	$50
450			450	

This leaves the purchases account with a debit balance of $500 and an allowance of $50, the amount of the voucher and the liability now being $450.

Is there any clue to this? There may be, but some memory is involved. When there is a return of merchandise after the voucher register has been posted, two recordings are to be made. First, debit Accounts Payable with the amount of the old voucher, credit Purchases Returns and Allowances with the amount of the return, and credit Purchases with the difference. Next, record the amount of the new voucher in the register.

Memory is fickle, reason is more reliable, so one should think along these lines: The amount of the original purchase should remain in the purchases account in order that the allowance may be subtracted from it on the profit and loss statement. The amount owed after the return should remain in the accounts payable account.

Chapter XXII

TAXES

AN ACCOUNTANT may work at his profession for years and seldom record some of the transactions he learned to record in the classroom. He could hardly work a week, however, without recording a payroll. An accountant's first job with large business firms quite often is in payrolls. Payroll accounting is therefore a must for anyone who contemplates a career in accounting.

Four things must be learned: the recording of a payroll, the recording of the employer's liability for payroll taxes, the recording of the payment of the liabilities, and the recording of an accrued payroll.

Each employer is furnished with an employer's tax guide by the Internal Revenue Service. In the guide will be found tables which indicate how much income tax is to be withheld from employees for weekly, biweekly, semimonthly, monthly, daily, or miscellaneous pay periods. In the guide will be found Federal Insurance Contributions Act (F.I.C.A.) tables also. The terms F.I.C.A. taxes, F.O.A.B. (Federal Old Age Benefit) taxes, and social security taxes are used interchangeably in accounting.

The social security tax rates change more often than new editions of accounting textbooks are printed, so one should not be too concerned if the textbook differs from the prevailing rates. Rates changes are always well publicized and a new tax guide is sent to every employer whenever there is a change in rates. The principles of payroll tax accounting are always the same regardless of the rates used. F.I.C.A. taxes now in law are: 1974–77, 5.85%; 1978–80, 6.05%; 1981–85, 6.15%; 1986–97, 6.25%.

To record a payroll:

Wages Expense		$2,400
Employee's Income Tax Payable		$ 400
F.I.C.A. Taxes Payable	5.85%	140.40
Cash		1,859.60

F.I.C.A. taxes are withheld from employees wages up to $13,200, which is the ceiling under the present law. The employer is liable for these taxes on the first $13,-200 paid in wages to each employee. In addition, if he has one or more employees, any of whom has worked one or more days in twenty different work weeks or has been paid $1,500 or more in any calendar quarter of a year, he is also liable for federal and state unemployment taxes totaling 3.2 percent on the first $4,200 paid to each employee. In order to keep up with this and to aid in making reports to governmental agencies a payroll record of each employee should be kept. There may be many other deductions (for bonds, hospital insurance, union dues, the Christmas party, etc.) besides those recorded in the illustration. If so, it would only mean more credits to the accounts involved and a smaller credit to cash.

Assuming a payroll of four or more employees, none of whom had been paid as much as $4,200 in this fiscal year, the employer's liability for payroll taxes would be recorded in the following manner:

Payroll Tax Expense		$217.20
F.I.C.A. Payable	5.85%	$140.40
F.U.T.A. Payable	0.5%	12.00
S.U.T.A. Payable	2.7%	64.80

A provision in the original Federal Unemployment Tax Act allowed the various states to keep up to 90 percent of the unemployment taxes if their legislatures passed an unemployment tax act. All of them did, of course. The 3 percent unemployment tax was divided—10 percent federal and 90 percent state, or 0.3 percent and 2.7

percent. (Now, however, the federal rate is 0.5 percent and the state rate 2.7 percent.) For a full employment record a state may give a merit rating to an employer that is lower than 2.7 percent.

If the income taxes withheld from employees plus the F.I.C.A. taxes withheld plus the employer's share of F.I.C.A. taxes come to as much as $100 in one month, the employer must deposit the money in a federal reserve-approved bank and obtain a depository receipt. The income taxes withheld and the liability for F.I.C.A. taxes are paid quarterly. Form 941, which lists the name of each employee, the total taxable wages, and the amount of the income taxes withheld, is prepared and a check sent to the district director of Internal Revenue along with the report. Assuming that the $2,400 payroll which has been recorded was for an entire quarter the entry to record the check is as follows:

Employee's Income Tax Payable	$400	
F.I.C.A. Taxes Payable	280.80	
Cash		$680.80

The $280.80 debit to F.I.C.A. Taxes Payable is due to the 5.85 percent withheld from employees in the first illustration, and the 5.85 percent employer's contribution which was recorded in the second illustration.

State unemployment taxes are paid quarterly, so this entry would be:

S.U.T.A. Payable	$64.80	
Cash		$64.80

Federal unemployment taxes are paid annually, so this liability of $12.00 remains open in the ledger. Since it is paid annually, it would not have to be recorded until the end of the year, but the accountant has less analyzing to do if he records the federal liability every time he records the state liability.

The liability for an accrued payroll is recorded as any other accrued expense, disregarding the payroll taxes. Payroll taxes are based on wages paid, not earned.

Wages Expenses	$600	
Wages Payable		$600

A person has begun to understand the recording of payroll taxes when he can solve a problem such as the one that follows:

Messrs. Black, Green, Brown, and White have been employed the entire year by the Acme Company. Their pay and income tax withheld per month are as follows:

$500—$50; 600—$70; $700—$80; $800—$90. Mr. Gray has worked only the last three months. His pay and withholding tax per month is $600—$60.

  a. Record payment of the payroll for the *third* quarter.

  b. Record the Acme Company's liability for payroll taxes, assuming that the company has no merit rating.

  c. Record the payment of all liabilities that should be paid at the end of the quarter.

By making a payroll record for each employee it can quickly be determined which ones have been paid $4,200 (unemployment taxes), and which ones have been paid $13,200 (F.I.C.A. taxes).

The payroll record for the employees would show that after the third quarter none had reached the 1974 maximum of $13,200 and all had surpassed the unemployment maximum of $4,200 except Mr. Gray, who has been employed only three months.

(a)

Wages Expenses	$9,600		
Employee's Income Taxes Payable		$1,050	
F.I.C.A. Taxes Payable		561.60	
Cash		7,988.40	

(b)

Payroll Tax Expense	$619.20	
F.I.C.A. Payable		$561.60
F.U.T.A. Payable 0.5% of $1,800 (Mr. Gray)		9.00
S.U.T.A. Payable 2.7% of $1,800 (Mr. Gray)		48.60

(c)

Employee's Income Taxes Payable	$1,050	
F.I.C.A. Taxes Payable	1,123.20	
Cash		$2,173.00
(mailed to district director of Internal Revenue Service)		

S.U.T.A. Payable	48.60	
Cash		48.60
(mailed to state department of taxation)		

Some states have a sales tax at the retail level and the merchant is expected to collect the tax, usually 2 or 3 percent, and to turn the amount of the collections over to the department of taxation. One method of handling the tax is to prepare a sales ticket or invoice which shows the sale and the tax separately, both cash and credit. A cash receipts and a sales journal with a column for sales taxes payable should be designed.

The entries in the sale journal on page 103 indicate that sales of merchandise taxable at 3 percent have been made to John Smith, and that non-taxable merchandise has been sold to Bill Green. The entries in the cash receipts journal on page 103 indicate that cash sales of taxable merchandise at 3 percent have been recorded, that John Smith has paid his bill (the tax on which had already been recorded when it was purchased on credit) and that non-taxable cash sales of $200 have been recorded.

If it is not expedient to record sales taxes payable on cash sales, they should be recorded together as sales and the sales tax column omitted from the cash receipts journal. The total cash receipts minus the total paid on account should give the amount of the cash sales and the tax combined. If the tax is 3 percent, this amount represents 103 percent. This amount is divided by 1.03 to obtain the amount of the sales. Three percent of the sales gives the tax.

All cash receipts for month		$1,333
Deduct: Total of Accounts Receivable		
credit column	$103	
Non-taxable sales	200	303
Total of cash sales and tax		$1,030
1,030 ÷ 1.03 =	1,000	
	.03	
	$30.00	

If many non-taxable sales were to be recorded, a separate column for these sales should be provided in the cash receipts journal in order to have this total to be subtracted. If the sales tax column had been omitted from the cash receipts journal, the $1,030 would have been recorded as a sale. After the tax had been determined by arithmetic as illustrated, Sales should be debited with $30, and Sales Tax Payable should be credited with $30.

For small businesses with little clerical help, still less red tape would be involved and simpler accounting would be obtained if the sales tax column was omitted from all journals. Then the total cash received during a month plus the credit sales minus the non-taxable sales would give the total taxable sales and the taxes combined. The taxes and the sales could be separated by arithmetic. When the check for sales taxes was mailed to the state department of taxation, sales should be debited and cash should be credited. When this procedure is followed, the liability for Sales Taxes Payable

CASH RECEIPTS JOURNAL

Date	Description	Posting Reference	Sales Credit	Sales Tax Payable Credit	Accounts Receivable Credit	Sales Discount Debit	Cash Debit
June 7	Sales for Week 1-7		$1,000	$30			$1,030
7	John Smith				$103		103
7	Non-taxable Sales		200				200

SALES JOURNAL

Date	Sold to:	Posting Reference	Accounts Receivable Debit	Sales Tax Payable Credit	Sales Credit
June 6	John Smith	✓	$103	$3	$100
10	Bill Green	✓	80		80

would be recorded only on the last day of the fiscal year. This entry should be reversed. The following illustrates this procedure.

Cash	$600	
Accounts Receivable	630	
Non-taxable Sales		$ 200
Taxable Sales		1,030
(To record sales for month of January)		
Taxable Sales	$ 30	
Cash		$ 30
(To record payment of sales taxes for January)		

The same type of entry would be made for each month through November. The following entries would be made for December:

Cash	$520	
Accounts Receivable	926	
Non-taxable Sales		$ 210
Taxable Sales		1,236
(To record sales for December)		
Taxable Sales	$ 36	
Sales Taxes Payable		$ 36
(To record sales tax liability for December)		
Sales Taxes Payable	$ 36	
Taxable Sales		$ 36
(To reverse the entry setting up the new balance sheet account, Sales Taxes Payable; entry dated January 1 as usual)		
Taxable Sales	$ 36	
Cash		$ 36
(To record payment of sales taxes in January the same way it is recorded the other eleven months)		

Some states allow the merchant a small percentage of the sales tax, 2 or 3 percent, for collecting it. Under these circumstances, the liability, Sales Tax Payable, may be discharged by paying a smaller amount which results in income for the merchant. Suppose the state sales tax is 3 percent and the merchant is given 2 percent of the tax for collecting it. If taxable sales for a month are $4,000 and the sales tax liability has been recorded, the balance of the account would be $120. The liability may be paid with a check for $117.60. The balance of the account may be closed into an account entitled Sales Tax Income or the sales account at the end of each month or at the end of the fiscal year.

In small businesses where the liability for sales taxes is not recorded monthly but is included in the sales account, the same procedure that has already been illustrated would obtain. After considering the merchant's percentage for collecting the tax, the amount owed to the state department of taxation is determined. A check is written for this amount and charged to Sales. This leaves the merchant's income from sales tax collections in the principal income account and no attempt is made to separate it.

The amount of the property taxes should be recorded at the end of a fiscal year by a debit to Property Tax Expense and a credit to Property Taxes Payable. Property taxes accrue and are paid after they are due.

The chief concern an accountant has with federal income taxes is the preparation of Schedule "C" which is in the form of a profit and loss statement. Personal income tax returns can usually be completed by following the instructions that are received with the form. All accounting is income tax accounting, but the theory of debit and credit does not necessarily apply in the preparation of tax returns. The prospective accountant should take all the courses in federal income taxes that he can.

A condensed version of this subject would be of so little value that it has been omitted in this book.

Chapter XXIII

DIVISION OF PARTNERSHIP PROFITS

A PARTNERSHIP IS AN association of two or more persons to carry on, as co-owners, a business for profit. A partnership is formed by drawing up a contract, Articles of Co-Partnership, in which is stated the salient features of the agreement, such as the name, place of business, nature of business, contributions to be made by partners, fiscal year, division of profits, and others. This contract may be oral, which is as legal as a written one. However, written contracts are easier to prove, which makes them more desirable.

One of the principal things to be learned in accounting for partnerships is division of profits. Some of the most common agreements on division of profits are equal shares, fixed ratio, investments, average capital, fixed ratio with interest on investments, and fixed ratio with salaries and interest on investments. If nothing is stated about division of profits in the partnership agreement, the profits and losses are divided equally.

As in a sole proprietorship, the nominal accounts are closed into the profit and loss summary (or income summary) and the balance of this account is closed into the partners' drawing or the partners' capital accounts. The direct method of closing the summary account into the capital accounts will be used in the illustrations.

Profit and Loss Summary

Total expenses $20,000	$26,000 Total income
	6,000 Balance

Assume that the expenses and incomes have been closed and the summary account has a credit balance of $6,000 which represents profit. Assume capital balances as follows:

John Doe, Capital		Bill Doe, Capital	
$15,000	Sept.1 $5,000	$10,000	
	Nov. 1 5,000	5,000	July 1
		5,000	Balance

If the division of profits is to be equal, the final closing entry is as follows:

Profit and Loss Summary	$6,000	
John Doe, Capital		$3,000
Bill Doe, Capital		3,000

If the division of profits is to be a fixed ratio of two to one, the final closing entry is as follows:

Profit and Loss Summary	$6,000	
John Doe, Capital		$4,000
Bill Doe, Capital		2,000

If the division of profits is to be in the ratio of the partners' ending capitals, the final closing entry is as follows:

Profit and Loss Summary	$6,000	
John Doe, Capital		$4,500
Bill Doe, Capital		1,500

If the division of profits is to be in the ratio of the partners' average capitals, the final closing entry is as follows:

Profit and Loss Summary	$6,000	
John Doe, Capital		$3,600
Bill Doe, Capital		2,400

Since John Doe's capital did not change during the year, his average capital is the same as the beginning capital, $15,000. Bill Doe's capital was $10,000 on January 1, so he had $10,000 in the account for six months. On July 1, he invested an additional $5,000, so he had $15,000 in the account for two months. On September 1, he withdrew $5,000, so he had $10,000 in the account for two months until he withdrew another $5,000, which made him have $5,000 in the account for the last two months. This information is expressed in this manner:

$$
\begin{array}{rcr}
\$10,000 \times 6 &=& \$60,000 \\
15,000 \times 2 &=& 30,000 \\
10,000 \times 2 &=& 20,000 \\
5,000 \times 2 &=& 10,000 \\
\hline
12 &) 120,000 (& 10,000
\end{array}
$$

The months should add up to twelve. Since the average capitals of the partners were $15,000 and $10,000, the $6,000 profit was divided in the ratio of three to two. If the division of profits is to be a fixed ratio of two to one with 6 percent on the beginning capital, the final closing entries are as follows:

Profit and Loss Summary	$1,500	
John Doe, Capital		$900
Bill Doe, Capital		600
(To give each partner 6 percent interest on beginning capital)		

Profit and Loss Summary	$4,500	
John Doe, Capital		$3,000
Bill Doe, Capital		1,500
(To give each partner his remaining share of profits at a fixed ratio of two to one)		

These computations may be made separately and the final closing entry made in one entry instead of two.

Profit and Loss Summary	$6,000	
John Doe, Capital		$3,900
Bill Doe, Capital		2,100

The latter entry would require more explanation and would make the auditor's work more difficult.

If the division of profits is to be a fixed ratio of one to one, with a salary to John Doe of $8,000, a salary of $4,000 to Bill Doe, and 6 percent interest on the ending capitals, the final closing entries are as follows:

Profit and Loss Summary	$12,000	
John Doe, Capital		$8,000
Bill Doe, Capital		4,000
(To give each partner salaries as per agreement)		

Profit and Loss Summary	$1,200	
John Doe, Capital		$900
Bill Doe, Capital		300
(To give each partner 6 percent interest on ending capitals)		

John Doe, Capital	$3,600	
Bill Doe, Capital	3,600	
Profit and Loss Summary		$7,200
(To distribute summary balance in ratio of one to one)		

As in the preceding illustration, the computations could have been made on a separate sheet of paper and one entry made instead of three.

Profit and Loss Summary	$6,000	
John Doe, Capital		$5,300
Bill Doe, Capital		700

When the profit and loss division agreement is complicated, such as interest on capitals, salaries, rent and a fixed ratio, one should not be concerned if the balance of the summary account becomes a debit because the balance of the summary account will be divided among the partners in a fixed ratio regardless of which side the balance is on. In the last illustration the summary account had a debit balance of $6,000 after the partners had been given $12,000 in salaries. It had a $7,200 debit after the partners had been given $1,200 in interest. This $7,200 was divided equally between the partners by the last entry illustrated.

Chapter XXIV

ADMISSION OF A NEW PARTNER

WHEN A NEW PARTNER is admitted to a partnership the old partnership is dissolved and a new partnership is formed from a legal standpoint. New Articles of Co-Partnership must be agreed upon and all the owners must consent to the admission of the new partner. Partners may be admitted in many ways, such as by purchase of an interest from an old partner, by investment, by transfer of a business, by payment of a bonus to the old partners, by recording goodwill as a benefit to the old partners, by a bonus to the new partner, and by recording goodwill as a benefit to the new partner.

Assume Jones Capital, $10,000 and Smith Capital, $10,000. Brown purchases one-fourth of the business, an equal amount from each of the old partners.

Jones, Capital	$2,500	
Smith, Capital	2,500	
Brown, Capital		$5,000

It is important to remember that the above entry would have been the same no matter what amount Brown paid the old partners for one-fourth of the business. Since the partners are receiving the money as individuals, the partnership net worth will remain the same even if Brown pays them $50,000.

The admission of Brown by an investment would be recorded as follows:

Cash	$5,000	
Brown, Capital		$5,000

The admission of Brown by the transfer of a business would be recorded as follows:

Cash	$ 5,000	
Assets	10,000	
Liabilities		$ 5,000
Brown, Capital		10,000

Assume White Capital, $6,000, and Black Capital, $8,000. Green invests $10,000 into the business for one-fourth interest.

Cash	$10,000	
Green, Capital		$10,000
Green, Capital	$4,000	
White, Capital		$2,000
Black, Capital		2,000

Green was willing for the old partners to receive this bonus because the business was making excess profits or had fine prospects for growth. The capital of the partnership before Green's entry was $14,000. After Green invests $10,000 cash into the partnership, the total capital is $24,000. Since Green is to receive one-fourth of the ownership of the business, his capital must be $6,000. Green's admission into the partnership could have been recorded with one entry as follows:

Cash	$10,000	
Green, Capital		$6,000
White, Capital		2,000
Black, Capital		2,000

When the new partner's ownership percentage differs from the amount of his investment, the best procedure is to give him credit for the amount of his investment and then to adjust his capital account to reflect the correct ownership agreement. The bonus of $4,000 in the preceding illustration was divided equally between White and Black because nothing was said about the profit and loss sharing agreement, so it had to be even. Profits will be divided equally in future illustrations.

If, in the preceding illustration, Green was willing to invest $10,000 for a one-fourth interest but was unwilling to have his capital account reduced below $10,000, his entry could have been recorded by the goodwill method. Goodwill is an intangible asset. It is defined as the value attached to a business over and above its actual, physical net worth. Green's entry into the partnership would be recorded by the goodwill method as follows:

Cash	$10,000	
Green, Capital		$10,000
Goodwill	$16,000	
White, Capital		$8,000
Black, Capital		8,000

After Green invests $10,000 into the business it is worth $24,000. If Green will not allow his capital to be reduced, his capital of $10,000 must represent one-fourth of the total capital. If $10,000 represents one-fourth, the total capital must be $40,000. Since the physical worth of the business is only $24,000, an intangible asset valued at $16,000 must be recorded.

Suppose Green invests $4,000 for one-third interest in the partnership. The entry:

Cash	$4,000	
Green, Capital		$4,000
White, Capital	$1,000	
Black, Capital	1,000	
Green, Capital		$2,000

This method of recording gives the new partner a bonus. After the investment of $4,000, the total capital was $18,000. One-third of eighteen is six, so Green receives a bonus of $2,000.

If the old partners agreed to let Green come in the business by investing $4,000 and owning one-third, but insisted upon no reduction of their capital accounts, the goodwill method of recording would have been used.

Cash	$4,000	
Green, Capital		$4,000
Goodwill	$3,000	
Green, Capital		$3,000

After Green's investment of $4,000 the total capital of the partnership was $18,000. Since the new partner was to own one-third of the business the old partners must own two-thirds. Their combined capital is $14,000. If $14,000 is two-thirds, one-third must be $7,000. Goodwill must be recorded at $3,000 to bring Green's capital up to $7,000.

The exact amount of the goodwill to be recorded in admitting a new partner can always easily be determined by using the fraction of ownership of either the new partner or the fraction of ownership of the old partners. In the first illustration of the goodwill method the new partner's capital of $10,000, representing one-fourth of the business, was used to determine what four/fourths would be. In the last illustration the old partners' capitals of $14,000, representing two-thirds, were used to determine what three/thirds would be. Either the new partner's capital will not change or the old partners' capitals will not change. The one that will not change should be used to determine the total capital. Then the amount of the goodwill can easily be determined by subtraction.

The bonus method of recording the admission of a new partner is more conservative and should be used if the accountant has a choice. If the new partner has a knowledge of accounting, he may insist upon the difference and vice versa. In the liquidation of a partnership an intangible asset such as goodwill will be a total loss. If the new partner shares less in the profits and losses than the old partners, he should be quite willing for his entry to be recorded by the goodwill method and in case of liquidation the greater loss would be shared by the old partners. If the new partner's share of profits and losses is greater than the old partners, he should insist that his entry be recorded by the bonus method. This would keep an intangible asset off the books which would be a total loss in liquidation, the greater share of which would be borne by the new partner.

Chapter XXV

WITHDRAWAL OF A PARTNER

AS IN THE ADMISSION of a new partner, the withdrawal of a partner causes the old partnership to be dissolved, and, if the business is to continue as a partnership, a new one is formed.

A partner may retire by having another partner or partners purchase his interest, by receiving from the partnership assets equal to his interest, by receiving from the partnership assets greater than his interest, or by receiving from the partnership assets less than his interest.

Assume White Capital $6,000, Black Capital $8,000, and Green Capital $10,000 with profits and losses shared equally. If it is agreed that Black will purchase Green's interest for $5,000 cash, the entry is as follows:

Green, Capital	$10,000	
Black, Capital		$10,000

This entry would have been made regardless of how much Black personally paid Green for his interest in the partnership.

If the partners agreed that the partnership would pay Green $12,000 to withdraw, the transaction would be recorded as follows:

Green, Capital	$10,000	
Black, Capital	1,000	
White, Capital	1,000	
Cash		$12,000

If partners Black and White objected to having their capital accounts reduced by this bonus method of recording, the transaction could be recorded by the goodwill method as follows:

Goodwill	$2,000	
Green, Capital		$2,000
Green, Capital	$12,000	
Cash		$12,000

The theory in this recording is that if the partners are willing to give the retiring partner $12,000 for his ownership interest of only $10,000 there must be intangible assets of $2,000. Taking this theory a bit further, the remaining partners could reason that the entire firm goodwill must be $6,000 since Green's share was $2,000 and profits are divided equally. To record the entire firm goodwill the entry would be:

Goodwill	$6,000	
Black, Capital		$2,000
White, Capital		2,000
Green, Capital		2,000
Green, Capital	$12,000	
Cash		$12,000

The entire firm goodwill is based upon the profit and loss sharing ratio. In the illustration, if Green's share had been 20 percent, and Black's and White's 40 percent each, the $2,000 extra he was given would be considered 20 percent of the goodwill. If one-fifth of the goodwill is $2,000, the total goodwill must be $10,000. The extra amount given to a retiring partner divided by the retiring partner's percentage of profits will give the entire firm goodwill. The bonus method of recording the above transactions would be more conservative, as it deals only with tangible assets.

If Green accepted only $8,000 for his ownership, the retirement of the partner would be recorded in this manner:

Green, Capital	$10,000	
Cash		$8,000
White, Capital		1,000
Black, Capital		1,000

This entry indicates the presence of negative goodwill, but no attempt is made to record it. If the partnership already had goodwill on its books, this account could be credited with $2,000 instead of White and Black. The reasoning behind the recording as illustrated is that liabilities and proprietorship are the same as far as a business is concerned. It does not care how the ownership of its net assets are divided. It reasons that if a liability can be paid by giving a creditor less than the debt, the business has gained. It also reasons that if the amount the business owes to a proprietor can be discharged by giving the proprietor less, the remaining proprietors have gained.

When a partner dies, the books of the partnership should be closed as of the date of death unless there is specific agreement otherwise. When the deceased partner's capital is determined it should be debited and a "payable to the estate of the deceased" account should be credited. The articles of co-partnership should stipulate the procedure in case of death of a partner.

Chapter XXVI

LIQUIDATION OF A PARTNERSHIP

A PARTNERSHIP may be dissolved by the admission or withdrawal of a partner, and a new partnership begun. A partnership may be dissolved and a new one begun without the public being aware that any change is taking place. When a partnership is liquidated it generally means that all liabilities are to be paid, the assets are to be sold, the partners are to be paid their remaining ownership interests, and the business is to cease to exist.

In liquidation all creditors must be paid before partners are paid. Gains and losses are incurred in selling the assets. These gains or losses may be recorded in an account entitled "loss or gain on asset realization," but since this account must be closed into the partner's capital accounts it has little value unless several assets are to be sold over a period of several months.

Assume a trial balance as follows:

Cash	$10,000	
Other Assets	50,000	
Liabilities		$36,000
White, Capital		6,000
Black, Capital		8,000
Green, Capital		10,000
	$60,000	$60,000

The profit and loss sharing ratio is 2:2:1. All the assets are sold for $60,000 cash. This would be recorded as follows:

Cash	$60,000	
Assets		$50,000
White, Capital		4,000
Black, Capital		4,000
Green, Capital		2,000

The liabilities are paid.

Liabilities	$36,000	
Cash		$36,000

The partners are paid.

White, Capital	$10,000	
Black, Capital	12,000	
Green, Capital	12,000	
Cash		$34,000

These entries close all of the partnership accounts. It should be noted particularly that the partners received cash according to their ownership or capital and not according to the profit or loss sharing agreement. In liquidation, profits or losses are distributed according to an agreed ratio, but assets (usually cash) are distributed according to their ownership. This important point must be remembered if difficulty in recording partnership liquidations is to be avoided.

Assume the same trial balance and profit and loss sharing agreement as before. All the assets are sold for $25,000.

Cash	$25,000	
White, Capital	10,000	
Black, Capital	10,000	
Green, Capital	5,000	
Assets		$50,000

After this entry is posted, the ledger appears as follows:

Cash		Liabilities		White, Capital	
$35,000			$36,000	$4,000	

		Black, Capital		Green, Capital	
		$2,000			$5,000

The debit balances in White's and Black's capital accounts are known as a "deficiency." The partnership has a claim against the partners and each of them has to pay the partnership the amount of his deficiency unless he is bankrupt. If both paid their deficiency, the final recording of the liquidation is as follows:

Cash	$4,000	
White, Capital		$4,000
Cash	2,000	
Black, Capital		2,000
Liabilities	36,000	
Cash		36,000
Green, Capital	5,000	
Cash		5,000

If either partner is bankrupt or the partnership is unable to collect his deficiency, that partner's debit balance must be absorbed by the other partners in the profit and loss sharing ratio. Assuming Black is unable to pay, the final liquidation is recorded as follows:

White, Capital	$1,333	
Green, Capital	667	
Black, Capital		$2,000
Cash	5,667	
White, Capital		5,667
Liabilities	36,000	
Cash		36,000
Green, Capital	4,333	
Cash		4,333

If the deficiency could not be collected from either partner, Green would have to invest $1,000 into the partnership in order to pay the liabilities in full. After Green's capital had been credited with the $1,000 investment and the other partners' debit balance had been closed into Green's capital account the ledger would be closed. If all the partners were bankrupt, the partnership would lack $1,000 of having enough to pay the creditors in full after all the cash had been applied toward paying the liabilities.

In actual practice it is almost impossible to liquidate a partnership all at once as in the previous illustrations. Unless the partnership is to bear undue losses the assets cannot be sold all at once, so the liquidation must take place over a period of time. Partners, being people, must withdraw cash from the partnership from time to time in order to provide for their families. The accountant charged with the recording of the liquidation must be extremely careful not to overpay a partner during this period. If a partner is paid more than he is entitled to during liquidation, it may become embarrassing to try to get the money back. In order to keep from overpaying a partner it must be assumed that all the remaining assets will be a total loss and the loss distributed in the profit and loss ratio. This will reduce the ownership equities to the amount of cash to be distributed and the accountant can see which of the partners owns the cash and if the cash is given to the partners according to who owns it, no one can be overpaid. In order to illustrate the preceding, assume that partners A, B, and C are liquidating. A's capital is $30,000, B's capital is $40,-000, and C's capital is $30,000. The profit and loss ratio is 2:2:1. All liabilities have been paid, which took all the cash, leaving assets of $100,000; $50,000 of assets are sold for $25,000. Record:

Cash	$25,000	
A, Capital	10,000	
B, Capital	10,000	
C, Capital	5,000	
Assets		$50,000

Since all liabilities have been paid, the partners agree to the distribution of $15,000 cash. Who is to get it? To keep from overpaying a partner, the capital accounts must be reduced to the $15,000 to be distributed. This cannot be done in the ledger proper without mutilating the records, so proceed according to these rules.

1. Prepare a work sheet of "T" accounts of all the accounts open in the ledger.

2. Consider all the assets a total loss except the cash to be distributed and distribute this loss to partners in the profit and loss sharing ratio.

3. If this loss distribution causes a partner's capital account to have a debit balance, distribute the debit balance to the partner's capital accounts with credit balances in the profit and loss sharing ratio.

4. If this distribution causes other debit balances to occur, close them into the ones with credit balances in the profit and loss sharing ratio.

To follow instruction number one, a work sheet of "T" accounts of all the accounts open in the ledger at the time of the distribution of $15,000 cash would be as follows:

Cash	Assets	A, Capital (2)	B, Capital (2)
$25,000	$50,000	$20,000	$30,000

	C, Capital (1)
	$25,000

The accounts on the work sheet should be checked to make sure they are in balance. If, in following instruction number two, all the assets are to be considered a total loss except the cash to be distributed and this loss distributed in the profit and loss sharing ratio, the work sheet would appear as follows:

Cash		Assets		A, Capital (2)	
$25,000	$10,000	$50,000	$50,000	$24,000	$20,000

B, Capital (2)		C, Capital (1)	
$24,000	$30,000	$12,000	$25,000

The distribution of the total possible loss of $10,000 cash and $50,000 assets in the profit and loss sharing ratio resulted in a debit balance of $4,000 in A's capital account. In distributing this loss to the partners with credit balances, according to instruction number three, the work sheet would appear as follows:

Cash		Assets		A, Capital (2)	
$25,000	$10,000	$50,000	$50,000	$24,000	$20,000
					4,000

B, Capital (2)		C, Capital (1)	
$24,000	$30,000	$12,000	$25,000
2,667		1,333	

The distribution of the debit balance of $4,000 in A's capital account did not make any more debit balances, so it can now be determined who gets the $15,000 by the credit balances in the capital accounts. B's capital has a credit balance of $3,333 and C's capital has a credit balance of $11,667. The journal entry to record the distribution of the cash is:

B, Capital	$ 3,333	
C, Capital	11,667	
Cash		$15,000

After another month or so of sales of assets there would be another distribution and the same process would be in order again. At any time during liquidation if the capital accounts reach the profit and loss ratio, cash may be distributed in that ratio from then on. This usually occurs by the third distribution.

Another method of determining the amount of cash to be distributed to partners without risking an overpayment is the use of a mathematical process to determine the loss that each partner is able to absorb.

Partner	Amt. of Capital	Profit & Loss Share		Loss to Absorb Equity
A	$30,000 ÷	.40	=	$ 75,000
B	40,000 ÷	.40	=	100,000
C	30,000 ÷	.20	=	150,000

Since partner C can stand a total loss of $50,000 more than anyone else, the first $10,000 in cash must be given to him. This is determined by multiplying C's excess loss capacity of $50,000 by .20. After partner C has received $10,000, the chart would appear as follows:

Partner	Amt. of Capital	Profit & Loss Share		Loss to Absorb Equity
A	$30,000 ÷	.40	=	$ 75,000
B	40,000 ÷	.40	=	100,000
C	20,000 ÷	.20	=	100,000

Since partner B and C's loss to absorb is now the same, the next cash paid to partners must be paid to them and in the ratio .40 to .20, or 2 to 1. Each of these two partners' loss to absorb is $25,000 more than A's, so 40 percent times $25,000 = $10,000, and 25 percent times $25,000 = $5,000. The next $15,000 in cash to be given to partners must be divided between B and C in the ratio of two to one. In the previous illustration, $15,000 was given to partners. Using this chart it would be figured in this way. The first $10,000 goes to C according to the first chart. Then $5,000 would be divided between B and C in the ratio of two to one, so B would receive $3,333 and C would receive $1,667 of this amount. Of the $15,000 to be distributed then the entry would be the same as in the previous illustration.

B, Capital	$ 3,333	
C, Capital	11,667	
Cash		$15,000

A new chart does not have to be made after each distribution of cash. It was done here only to make the explanation clearer. When cash is distributed a subtraction needs to be made from the Loss to Absorb and that is all. Using this method the partners can be told in advance how the cash will be distributed so each will be able to understand the process of distribution. In this illustration the partners should be given the following program of distribution:

The first $10,000 is to be given to C.

The next $15,000 is to be divided between B and C in the ratio of two to one.

Any remaining cash is to be distributed to partners in the profit sharing ratio.

This method is considered more advanced than the first method, but it is probably easier to understand and certainly requires less work. In addition, all parties know what is going on during a period of liquidation.

Sometimes a priority list of payments in the liquidation of partnerships is given as follows: First, pay creditors; second, pay partners' loans; third pay partners' capitals. This only means that in liquidation a partner's loan and his capital should be considered together in determining his total capital. When it is determined that a partner is to receive cash his loan account should be charged first and any amounts remaining should be charged to his capital account. To avoid confusion the partners' loan accounts could be closed into their capital accounts at the beginning of liquidation.

Chapter XXVII

THE CORPORATE ORGANIZATION

A CORPORATION is an artificial being, invisible, intangible, and existing only in contemplation of law. This is Chief Justice John Marshall's definition which he gave in 1819. As an artificial being it has to pay taxes on its income as other beings do.

The principal difference in accounting for a sole proprietorship, a partnership and a corporation is in the proprietorship accounts. Most transactions are recorded the same way for all three. Since most textbooks present the sole proprietorship, partnership and corporation in that order, sometimes one may get the idea that the degree of difficulty increases as he progresses from one type to the other. The difficulty in record-keeping depends upon the volume and the variety of the transactions. It would be easier to keep records for a very small corporation than for a very large sole proprietorship.

In the sole proprietorship the profit and loss summary account is closed into the owner's capital account. In a partnership it is closed into two or more capital accounts, and in a corporation it is closed into an account called "earned surplus or retained earnings." When there are thousands of owners of a business, as in a corporation, it is next to impossible to divide the profits among them, so the total profit is lumped together in one account. These profits are given out to the owners in the form of dividends.

The ownership of a corporation is evidenced by stock certificates. When stock is purchased, a stock certificate is received for each one hundred shares, or each fraction thereof. If four hundred and ten shares of stock were purchased, five certificates would be sent to the purchaser or his broker.

Stock is classified into two principal classes, common and preferred. Common is usually the voting stock and preferred is non-voting. In some instances, however, preferred stock has voting rights. Common stockholders receive dividends only after the preferred stockholders are paid. Common stock may be more desirable than preferred and vice versa. If a small corporation has $1,000 of 5 percent preferred stock and $1,000 of common stock and wishes to distribute $2,000 in dividends, the preferred stockholders would receive $50 ($1,000 at 5 percent) and the common stockholders would receive $1,950. If the same corporation had $60 to declare in dividends, the preferred shareholders would receive $50 and the common shareholders $10. If the preferred stock receives an additional rate above the regular rate, it is participating. Sometimes a preferred dividend is passed (not declared). These dividends in arrears must be paid before the common stockholders are paid if the preferred is cumulative.

A share of stock has several different values. Par value is the amount stated on the stock certificate. Market value is the last known sale price of stock or the amount someone has bid for the stock. Book value is the value allotted to a class of stock divided by the number of shares the stockholders own. Book value of stock is explained fully in Chapter XXXI.

Elaborate schemes for changing a partnership to a corporation have been devised. If the partnership is to continue with the same owners as principals, it is quite possible that the same books of account may be continued in use. The only entry needed in such a case is to change the capital accounts to capital stock.

Assets	Liabilities	A, Capital	B, Capital
$100,000	$40,000	$35,000	$25,000

Suppose the above partnership is to be changed into a corporation. A agrees to accept $35,000 in common stock and B agrees to accept $25,000. C has agreed to purchase $20,000 worth of common stock. If the same books are to be used, the only entry needed is to debit Cash $20,000, debit A Capital $35,000, debit B Capital $25,000 and credit Common Stock $80,000. If the partnership books are to be closed and new books opened for the corporation, it is almost as simple. To close any set of books the accounts with credit balances should be debited and the accounts with debit balances should be credited. Nothing could be simpler or more effective. To open a new set of books for the corporation, the accounts with debit balances should be debited and those with credit balances should be credited. Valuation accounts, such as allowance for depreciation and bad debts, do not complicate the situation. The entry to open the corporation ledger follows:

Assets	$100,000	
Liabilities		$40,000
Common Stock		60,000
(To transfer partnership assets and		
liabilities to the corporation)		
Cash	20,000	
Common Stock		20,000
(To record sale of common		
stock for cash)		

Often the partnership assets are revalued before its ledger is closed. When several assets are to be reevaluated, an account entitled "asset revaluations," or "loss or gain on revaluation of assets," is used in order not to have to divide the losses and gains to the partners' capital accounts so many times. If twenty assets are to be revalued, it would be simpler to debit or credit the assets and debit or credit the revaluation account than to divide the gains or losses each time a revaluation was recorded. After all twenty of the assets were revalued, the "asset revaluations" account would be closed into the partner's capital accounts in the profit and loss ratio. This would make one division of profits instead of twenty. The revaluation account would have little value for use in a sole proprietorship because there is no profit or loss division.

Corporations are taxed at the rate of 22 percent on the first $25,000 of profits and at the rate of 48 percent for all profits over $25,000. These federal income taxes cannot be considered an expense of the corporation. Internal Revenue shares the profits as a partner. This is shown on the work sheet given on page 129.

The final closing entry is to debit Profit and Loss Summary $100,000, and credit Federal Income Taxes Payable $45,650 and Earned Surplus or Retained Earnings $54,350. For corporations the 10 percent increase in income taxes passed by Congress in 1968 is retroactive to January 1. This adds $4,150 to the taxes.

	Trial Balance	Adjustments	Profit and Loss		Balance Sheet	
			$100,000	$200,000		
Federal Income Taxes Payable			45,650*		$46,650	
Net Profit to Surplus			54,350		54,350	

$$
\begin{array}{rcl}
* \quad .22 \times \$25,000 &=& \$\ 5,500 \\
.48 \times 75,000 &=& 36,000 \\
\hline
\text{Total (1967)} &=& 41,500 \\
.10 \times 41,500 &=& 4,150 \\
\hline
\text{Total (1968)} &=& 45,650 \\
\end{array}
$$

Chapter XXVIII

CAPITAL STOCK

IN THE FORMATION of a corporation it is necessary to present to the Secretary of State sufficient proof that adequate capital can be raised. This is done by obtaining subscriptions to the capital stock. When a charter is received, the amount of capital stock authorized should be recorded. It may be recorded by a memorandum entry in the general journal, or the unissued and authorized capital stock may be recorded into the accounts. Both methods are illustrated.

1	2
Received a charter granting right to issue 1,000 shares of common stock, par $100, and 1,000 shares of preferred, 6%, par $100	Unissued Com. St. 100,000 Authorized Com. St. 100,000 Unissued Pref. St. 100,000 Authorized Pref. St. 100,000
Subscribed Rec. Com. 21,000 Com. Stock Subscribed 20,000 Prem. on Com. St. 1,000 (To record subscriptions to 200 shares at 110)	Same entry as #1
Cash 21,000 Subscribed Rec. Com. 21,000 (To record payment to subscriptions)	Same entry as # 1

Com. St. Subscribed   20,000
   Common Stock   20,000
	Com. Stock Subscribed 20,000
	   Unissued Com. Stock 20,000

The amount of stock that a corporation may issue is important information and should be shown on its balance sheet. If the memorandum method is used, the amount of authorized capital stock must be shown by a footnote. If the second method is used, this information is on the balance sheet and no footnote is needed. The proprietorship section of a balance sheet for both methods is illustrated.

Common Stock	$ 20,000	Authorized Com. St. $100,000	
Prem. on Com.	1,000	Less: Unissued Com.	80,000
Total Capital	21,000	Com. St. Outstanding	20,000
*Authorized Com.	$100,000	Premium on Com.	1,000
Authorized Pref.	100,000		
		Authorized Pref. St. 100,000	
		Less: Unissued Pref: 100,000	
		Total Capital	21,000

Premium on stock is classified as a capital or paid-in surplus account. It increases the total capital. If the stock in the preceding illustration was subscribed for at $19,000, a discount on common stock would have been recorded. This account decreases total capital.

Sometimes a subscriber will default after paying part of his subscription. When this happens, the corporation has four courses to take. It may give the money back, it may keep the money, it may sell the forfeited stock and settle with the defaulting subscriber, or it may issue a pro rata part of the stock. Suppose a subscription is received for preferred stock, par value $2,000 for $2,-100. The subscriber pays $600 on the subscription and then defaults. At this point the accounts appear as follows:

Cash	Subs. Rec. Pref.	Pref. St. Subs.	Prem. on Pref. St.
$600	$2,100 | $600	$2,000	$100

When a subscriber defaults, the accounts having anything to do with the transaction should be closed except the cash collected and a liability to the subscriber recorded. The entry:

Preferred Stock Subscribed	$2,000	
Premium on Preferred Stock	100	
Subscriptions Receivable Preferred		$1,500
Payable to Subscriber		600

After the liability to the defaulting subscriber has been set up, it is easy to record its disposition depending upon which of the four choices is chosen. If the corporation decides to give the money back to the subscriber, the entry is as follows:

Payable to Subscriber	$600	
Cash		$600

If the corporation decides to keep the money, the entry is:

Payable to Subscriber	$600	
Surplus from Forfeited Stock		$600

If the corporation decides to sell the stock again and then settle with the subscriber, the entry is:

Preferred Subscriptions Receivable	$2,050	
Payable to Subscriber	50	
Preferred Stock Subscribed		$2,000
Premium on Preferred Stock		100

In recording the subscription again at less than the original, the same premium should be recorded and the difference charged to the defaulting subscriber. If the corporation was fortunate enough to get a subscription of $2,200, the premium of $200 would be recorded and the $600 returned to the subscriber. To issue a pro rata amount of stock, the entry should be recorded as follows:

Payable to Subscriber	$500	
Preferred Stock		$500
Payable to Subscriber	25	
Premium on Preferred		25
Payable to Subscriber	75	
Cash		75

The posting of these entries leaves a balance in Cash of $525, Preferred Stock $500 and Premium on Preferred $25. If the premium on $2,000 of stock was $100, then the premium on $500 of stock should be $25. This is because the par value of the stock was $100 per share. Whatever the par value, the premium is 5 percent. If the par was $10, the premium would be $0.50. In this case 57 shares could be issued and the entry would be:

Payable to Subscriber	$570	
Preferred Stock		$570
Payable to Subscriber	28.50	
Premium on Preferred		28.50
Payable to Subscriber	1.50	
Cash		1.50

Ten people subscribe to ten shares each to be paid for in four equal installments and all of them pay the first installment, all pay the second, all pay the third, and only one person pays the fourth installment. If stock is issued to the fully paid subscribers, ten shares will be issued.

If a subscription of a number of subscribers has been recorded as a combined entry and one of the subscribers defaults later, it is a good idea to record the subscription of the defaulting subscriber on a separate sheet of paper in "T" accounts. It can easily be seen what has taken place in order for the proper amounts to be closed and the liability to the subscriber set up. For instance, if subscriptions to 2,000 shares of common, par $100, have been recorded in a combined entry at 105 and after a few installments were met, a subscriber to 20 shares defaults, the best procedure is to record in "T" accounts on scrap paper the subscription to 20 shares at 105 and the receipt of each payment. The liability to the subscriber is easy to visualize after this separate recording.

The corporate type of business is the most expensive to organize. Charter fees, lawyers fees, the cost of printing stock certificates and promotional expenses sometimes amount to substantial sums. In order to keep the baby corporation from being born with a deficit, these necessary organizational expenses are capitalized. These expenses are charged to an intangible asset, Organization Cost. This account is usually amortized over the first few years of its life, although theoretically it should be amortized over the entire life of the corporation. Since 1954, Internal Revenue has allowed this amortization charge to be considered an expense for income tax purposes. Formerly the charge was to Earned Surplus, or Retained Earnings.

When a corporation is authorized to issue no-par stock, the authorization is recorded by a memorandum entry. A sale of no-par stock is recorded in the no-par common stock account at the exact amount received, with no discount or premium recorded. A sale of no-par stock, 1,000 shares at 11 is recorded in this manner:

| Cash | $11,000 | |
| No-Par Common Stock | | $11,000 |

Some states allow a corporation's board of directors to place a "stated" value on no-par stock. In this situation, the sale of no-par stock is recorded in the same manner as stock with par value.

Chapter XXIX

DIVIDENDS

A THOROUGH understanding of the division of dividends among stockholder groups is highly important to anyone who plans to delve into accounting. Its importance is not derived from the fact that the accountant may have to participate in a management decision concerning dividends in the distant future, but from the fact that principles are involved that make the learning of more advanced accounting problems much easier. Two rough spots that become smooth with a thorough understanding of dividend division are the determination of book values of stocks when the preferred is cumulative and participating, and the elimination of the investment in a subsidiary in the preparation of consolidated balance sheets when the parent company owns a percentage of the subsidiary's common and preferred stocks.

In the distribution of dividends, par value is very important. If the preferred stock is participating, the preferred stockholders will participate in the dividend distribution above the stipulated rate in the ratio of the preferred par to the common par. Six percent preferred means the stockholder is to receive 6 percent of the preferred par value in one year before the common stockholders receive anything.

The participation of the preferred may be limited to a percentage of its par value, such as 10 percent. In such a case if the par value of the preferred was $100, the holder of one share could not receive more than $10 in dividends.

135

Suppose $30,000 in dividends are to be distributed in each of the following cases. The corporation has 3,000 shares of 6 percent preferred, par $100, and 4,000 shares of common, no-par. Each share would entitle a common stockholder to $3 and a preferred stockholder to $6. The $100 par multiplied by 6 percent is $6. There are 3,000 shares of preferred, so this takes $18,000. Since the preferred is non-cumulative and non-participating the remaining $12,000 is to be distributed to the common stockholders. There are 4,000 common shares which would entitle the owner of each share to $3. If it can be determined what one share entitles the owner to, it becomes relatively easy to determine the amount to which the holder of any number of shares is entitled.

The corporation has 2,500 shares of 7 percent participating preferred stock, par $100, and 1,500 shares of common, par $100. Each share would entitle the owner to $7.50. The par values are the same, so they will participate to the same extent after 7 percent has been given to each. There are 4,000 shares in all and $30,000 to be distributed, giving $7.50 to the holder of each share. At any time it can be seen that some further participation is to take place, the total number of shares may be divided into the amount to be distributed if the par values are the same. Until experience is gained in the distribution of dividends, no short cuts should be taken as in the above solution. The first step is to multiply the preferred par by its percentage. Thus, $100 multiplied by 7 percent is $7. Each preferred share is entitled to $7 and there are 2,500 shares. This takes $17,500 from the $30,000 to be distributed, leaving $12,500. The common par is $100 also, so each of the common shares is entitled to $7. There are 1,500 common shares, so this will take $10,500, leaving $2,000 out of the original $30,000. Each class of stock participates equally in the $2,000 since the pars are equal. There are 4,000 shares in all, so fifty cents per share is available. Fifty cents added to the $7 each share is entitled to make a total of $7.50.

The corporation has 2,500 shares of 6 percent preferred, par $100, and 2,500 shares of common, par $100. The holder of one share of each class of stock would receive $6. The par value of the preferred multiplied by 6 percent gives $6; $6 times 2,500 shares gives $15,000. The common par is $100, also entitling each share to $6; $6 times 2,500 common shares gives $15,000 which takes the entire $30,000. In this instance if the preferred had been participating, each share would entitle the holder to $6, because after each class of stock receives $6 there is nothing left in which to participate.

The corporation has outstanding 1,000 shares of preferred stock, 6 percent, cumulative, one year in arrears, par $100. It has 3,000 shares of common stock, par $50. Each share of preferred would entitle the holder to $12 and each share of common would entitle the holder to $6. One year in arrears means one year beside the current year. Last year the preferred dividend was passed and at the end of the next year, $30,000 are to be distributed in dividends.

Preferred

Par $100 x .06 = $6 x 1,000 shares = $6,000 (For the year in arrears)

Par $100 x .06 = $6 x 1,000 shares = $6,000 (For the current year)

$12 $12,000

Common

$30,000 — 12,000 = $18,000 ÷ 3,000 shares = $6

If the word "participating" is added to the last problem, it becomes as complex as any problem in dividend distribution, because the par values are not the same and the preferred is both cumulative and participating. Under these circumstances, a preferred share would entitle the holder to $15.60, and a common share would entitle the holder to $4.80.

Preferred

Par $100 x .06 = $6 x 1,000 shares = $6,000 (For the year in arrears)

Par $100 x .06 = $6 x 1,000 shares = $6,000 (For the current year)

Common

If the preferred share with a par value of $100 is entitled to $6 for the current year, a common share with a par value of $50 is entitled to $3 for the current year ——$3 x 3,000 shares = $9,000.

The $12,000 for the preferred and the $9,000 for the common leaves $9,000 to be distributed between the stockholders due to the participation clause. The total number of shares cannot be divided into the $9,000 in this problem because the par values are not the same. A common denominator must be used in order to determine the degree of participation of either the common or the preferred shares.

A thousand of the $100 shares is equal to 2,000 of the $50 shares; 3,000 of the common $50 par shares plus the 2,000 equivalent preferred shares gives 5,000— $9,000 ÷ 5,000 = $1.80. Each $50 par share will participate in the amount of $1.80, so each $100 par share will participate in the amount of $3.60.

Preferred		Common	
$ 6	(For the year in arrears)	$3	(For the current year)
6	(For the current year)	1.80	(Reduced to this amount due to participating preferred)
3.60	(Due to participating clause)		
$15.60		$4.80	

If the par values of the common and the preferred stocks are not the same and there is a participating amount to be distributed between them, the number of shares may be increased to the equivalent of the lower par or decreased to the equivalent of the higher par, whichever is easier. In the preceding illustration a common denominator of $100 pars could have been used. Thus, 3,000 shares of $50 pars is the equivalent of 1,500 shares of $100 pars; 1,000 shares of the preferred pars plus the 1,500 equivalent shares of common equals 2,500 shares—$9,000 ÷ 2,500 = $3.60 (the extra amount of a $100 par share).

There are three important dates involved in a dividend declaration, the date the board of directors declares the dividend, the date of stockholders' record, and the date of payment. A dividend becomes a liability once it is declared by the board of directors. Dividends in arrears are not a liability, but this is an important footnote on the balance sheet. The recording of the dividend should be made on the declaration date.

Earned Surplus	$10,000	
Dividends Payable		$10,000

The date of stockholders record is important because the dividend checks are mailed to the people who owned the stock at the close of business on that day. Stocks that are traded on the exchanges and over-the-counter trade ex-dividend four days prior to the date of the stockholders record because this is the average time it takes to complete a stock transfer. Checks are mailed on the date of payment and the following entry is recorded:

Dividends Payable	$10,000	
Cash		$10,000

If the corporation has both common and preferred stock, the liabilities for dividends should be labeled "common dividend payable" and "preferred dividend payable."

A corporation may find itself with plenty of earned surplus (or retained earnings) and very little cash. It may decide to pay a stock dividend when this situation arises. Suppose that a corporation has $100,000 in common stock, par $100, and $100,000 in earned surplus. It has a good cash position but plans to expand its facilities by purchasing new machinery or by an addition to the building. The entries to record and pay a stock dividend ($50,000 par, with a fair market value of $50,-000) follow:

Earned Surplus	$50,000	
Common Stock Dividend Payable		$50,000
Common Stock Dividend Payable	50,000	
Common Stock		50,000

The stock dividend recorded is a one for two dividend. One share of stock would be mailed to each stockholder for every two shares he owned. The payment of this dividend would decrease the market price of the stock by approximately one-third. Each stockholder would now have three shares where he formerly had two, but his percentage of ownership of the corporation would be the same. If the market price per share was $90 before the dividend, after the dividend the market would open at about $60 for this stock. Two shares were formerly worth $180 and after the dividend three shares are worth $180.

If, in the illustration, the market price of the stock was above or below par, Earned Surplus would be charged with the market value, Common Stock Dividend Payable credited with the par value and Premium on Common Stock credited or discount on common stock debited with the amount above or below par.

A corporation may split its stock to accomplish the same results as a stock dividend. A stock dividend caused some shifting of the balances of the earned surplus and common stock accounts, but the total of the two was still the same. A stock split-up leaves the balances in these accounts the same as they were before the split. A stock split of two for one would be recorded by a memorandum entry in the general journal. Using the same corporation as an illustration, the 1,000 old $100 par shares would be called in and 2,000 new $50 par shares would be mailed to stockholders to take their place. The stockholders are made very happy although they only have more paper and the same percentage of ownership of the company.

There are some advantages to stock splits and stock dividends or else there would not be so many of them. A price range of $30 to $50 is considered ideal by some analysts. If the price of a company's stock reaches $100 and over, it becomes out of the reach of thousands of stockholders. Stocks are traded in round lots of 100 and $10,000 is a lot of money for the average stockholder. If a purchaser wished to purchase less than 100 shares, his own broker must make the purchase through an odd-lot broker. This raises the purchasing price ⅛ per share because the odd-lot broker must purchase 100 shares and dispose of the fraction not purchased in any manner he can. The ⅛ is his cushion. This ⅛ will probably be negotiated in the future. A stock split of three for one will bring the price down to a more suitable level and enlarge the number of potential buyers. It will increase the number of people that can purchase in round lots. Stock dividends make for stockholder satisfaction and good stockholder relations. Many stockholders prefer a stock dividend to a cash dividend because they think more shares mean more value. Some more astute stockholders prefer stock dividends because they do not make the company worth less and cash dividends do.

A stock may be split down as well as up. If a stock is trading in the pennies, it may be made to look more respectable if the market price can be made to be over a dollar. The stockholders may approve a split of one for ten, in which the company sends the stockholders one share of stock, par $1, for each ten shares, par ten cents, that he owns. If the market price was fifty cents before the split, the price should be approximately $5 after the split. Approximate prices must be used in any illustration of market prices because nothing determines market price except the supply and demand. When a buyer makes a bid which is identical with an "asked" price, the stock and the money change hands.

The stock used for dividends and splits is usually common stock. Stock dividends and splits (up or down) are not considered income or expense for income tax purposes. Stock Dividends Payable should not be classified as a liability. It should appear under the common stock heading on the balance sheet.

Chapter XXX

TREASURY STOCK

TREASURY STOCK is stock that has been issued and reacquired by a corporation. One way that stock may be reacquired is by gift. The entry:

Treasury Stock	$10,000	
Donated Surplus		$10,000

The debit to Treasury Stock may be made at par or at market value. When the stock is sold, entries similar to the following are made:

Cash	$12,000	
Treasury Stock		$10,000
Donated Surplus		2,000
Cash	9,000	
Donated Surplus	1,000	
Treasury Stock		10,000

An accepted method is to record the donation of stock by a memorandum entry and to record only when sold.

The result would be the same. In the illustrations, if the memorandum method was used, the entry when sold would be:

Cash	$12,000	
Donated Surplus		$12,000
Cash	9,000	
Donated Surplus		9,000

Treasury stock may also be acquired by purchase. The purchase may be recorded on a cost basis or on a retirement basis. The latter basis considers the purchase of the stock as a temporary retirement.

The company purchases for $13,000 100 shares of its own common stock, par $100, which had originally been issued at 120. On the cost basis the following entry should be made:

Treasury Stock	$13,000	
Cash		$13,000

Treasury stock purchased at cost must be shown on the balance sheet as a deduction from its equity as follows:

Common Stock	$60,000	
Premium on Common Stock	10,000	$70,000
Less: Treasury Stock		13,000
Total Paid-In Capital		57,000

Sales of the above treasury stock would be recorded as follows:

Cash	$14,000	
Treasury Stock		$13,000
Treasury Stock Surplus		1,000
Cash	12,000	
Treasury Stock Surplus	1,000	
Treasury Stock		13,000

Purchase of the above stock at $13,000 would be recorded on the retirement basis as follows:

Treasury Stock	$10,000	
Premium on Common Stock	2,000	
Earned Surplus	1,000	
Cash		$13,000

If the company had paid $11,000 for the stock, it would have been recorded on the retirement basis as follows:

Treasury Stock	$10,000	
Premium on Common Stock	2,000	
Cash		$11,000
Paid-In Surplus on Stock Retirement		1,000

If either of these purchases of treasury stock is sold, it is recorded as if the stock had never been issued with the exception of a credit to Treasury Stock instead of Common Stock. The following entry records the sale of the treasury stock at $11,000 no matter what the stock cost the company:

Cash	$11,000	
Treasury Stock		$10,000
Premium on Common Stock		1,000

If the stock had been sold at $9,000, a discount of $1,000 would have been recorded.

Assume that the $10,000 of preferred stock sold at a premium of $2,000 is being redeemed and permanently retired. Sample recordings follow:

Preferred Stock	$10,000	
Premium on Preferred Stock	2,000	
Earned Surplus	1,000	
Cash		$13,000

Preferred Stock	10,000	
Premium on Preferred Stock	2,000	
Cash		11,000
Surplus from Stock Retirement		1,000

The first recording considers the redemption as a distribution of earnings because $13,000 was paid for stock which had been sold for $12,000. The second recording considers the redemption as a retention of capital, since only $11,000 was paid for stock that originally sold for $12,000.

As can be seen, some memory work is involved in recording the purchase of treasury stock and the retirement of preferred stock. A comparison of the entries will reduce the memory work to a minimum, however. To record the purchase of treasury stock on the cost basis, record it at the cost price. When sold for more or less than it cost, debit or credit Treasury Stock Surplus for the difference. On the retirement basis treasury stock is recorded at par when purchased, and premium or discount closed. If the purchase price is more than the issuing price, charge the difference to Earned Surplus. If the difference is less, credit the amount to Paid-In Surplus from Stock Retirement. When treasury stock that has been recorded on the retirement basis is sold it is recorded as if it were being sold for the first time with one exception—credit Treasury Stock instead of Capital Stock.

Treasury stock that has been recorded on the retirement basis may be subtracted from the stock account on the balance sheet since par is used in recording the purchase. Treasury stock should never be classified as an asset.

Many states permit the purchases of treasury stock up to the amount of the company's earned surplus only. If the earned surplus is $50,000, the corporation is permitted to purchase $50,000 of its stock. The earned surplus up to the amount of the treasury stock may not be declared in dividends. For this reason earned surplus up to the amount of treasury stock should be appropriated by a debit to the earned surplus account and a credit to an account entitled "reserve for treasury stock."

Chapter XXXI

BOOK VALUES OF STOCK

THE BOOK VALUE per share of stock is an important measurement of the owners' interest in a corporation. This knowledge would enable anyone to make more intelligent investments. The book value helps to determine the price that investors will pay for stock. It is the value of each share if the corporation liquidated and all assets realized their book value. The book value is easy to calculate if there is only one class of stock. The total capital divided by the number of shares outstanding gives this value.

When a corporation has both common and preferred stock, the common equity and the preferred equity must be determined and these amounts divided by the number of shares of each to determine book value.

Common Stock, $100 Par, 1,000 shares	$100,000
Preferred Stock, $100 Par, 1,000 shares	100,000
Earned Surplus (Retained Earnings)	100,000

What is the book value per share of the common and preferred in the above balance sheet? It depends upon the preferences of the preferred stock. Assuming that it is not preferred as to assets in liquidation, a few rules will suffice.

1. If the preferred is non-cumulative and non-participating, all the surplus or deficit is identified with the common equity.

2. If the preferred is cumulative, dividends in arrears are identified with the preferred equity, and the remainder of Earned Surplus or Deficit is identified with the common equity.

3. If the preferred is participating, or cumulative and participating, the Earned Surplus is identified with each stock equity as if it were to be given out in dividends. If there is a deficit, there would be no dividends, but dividends in arrears would still be identified with the preferred stock.

4. A deficit is identified with common stock in all cases except when the preferred stock is cumulative or cumulative-participating. In this case dividends in arrears are identified with the preferred and the remainder of the deficit is identified with the common.

The book value per share of stock according to rule number one is obtained as follows:

Preferred Stock

$100,000 ÷ 1,000 shares = $100 book value per share

Common Stock

$100,000 + Surplus identified with Common $100,000 = $200,000 ÷ 1,000 shares = $200 book value per share

It can readily be seen that if the preferred is plain, ordinary preferred, the book value is the same as the par value.

To illustrate rule number two, assume 6 percent preferred, two years in arrears, not including the current year.

Preferred Stock

$100,000 + $18,000 ($6,000 for each year in arrears plus the current year) = $118,000 ÷ 1,000 Shares = $118 book value per share

Common Stock

$200,000 − $18,000 = $182,000 ÷ 1,000 shares = $182 book value per share

In the illustration of rule number two if there had been only $10,000 of earned surplus instead of $100,000, the book values would have been determined as follows:

Preferred Stock

$118 book value per share (same manner as before)

Common Stock

$100,000 − $8,000 (deficit due to identifying $18,000 surplus with the preferred when the corporation only had $10,000) = $92,000 ÷ 1,000 shares = $92 book value per share

Proof:

Book value $118 x 1,000 shares preferred = $118,000
Book value $92 x 1,000 shares common = 92,000
    Combined equity $210,000

To illustrate rule number three, add "participating" to the previous problem. The earned surplus is allocated to the classes of stock as it would be if the entire surplus of $100,000 was declared as a dividend.

	Preferred	Common
Stock	$100,000	$100,000
First year in arrears	6,000	
Second year in arrears	6,000	
Current year	6,000	6,000
Dividend participation	38,000	38,000
	1,000)$156,000	1,000)$144,000
Book value per share	$156	$144

After allotting $18,000 to the preferred for two years in arrears and the current year, and after allotting $6,000 to the common for the current year, $76,000 remained to be distributed equally since the number of shares and the par value are the same for both the common and the preferred.

Chapter XXXII

CORPORATE BONDS

A BOND is a written promise, under seal, to pay a definite sum of money at a stated time and to pay interest at a stipulated rate. If the two words "under seal" were eliminated, the definition would be that of a note. The seal is a hangover from the time when many people could not write and important documents were stamped with a seal to establish their authenticity. The seal of the corporation should be placed on bonds; but if the corporation has no seal, the letters "L. S." should be written instead (*Locus Sigilli*—in place of the seal).

Fixed assets are usually pledged for both the face of the bonds and the interest, although debenture bonds may be issued on the general credit of the corporation.

Bonds are sometimes sold at more than face value because the interest on the bonds is higher than the prevailing rate at the time. The face of a bond is similar to the par value of preferred stock. It is the amount on which the interest is paid. If bonds, face value $100,000, 6 percent, are sold for $105,000, the transaction would be recorded as follows:

Cash	$105,000	
Bonds Payable		$100,000
Premium on Bonds Payable		5,000

Since the bond premium has been received because the rate of interest to be paid is higher than the prevailing rate, the premium is considered a deferred credit which is a liability classification. This liability should be amortized (killed; written off) over the life of the bonds. At the end of one year the entry to record payment of the bond interest would be:

Bond Interest Cost	$6,000	
Cash		$6,000

Assuming the life of the bonds to be five years the entry to amortize the premium using the straight-line method would be:

Premium on Bonds Payable	$1,000	
Bond Interest Cost		$1,000

These entries make the bond interest expense $5,000 for each year of life of the bonds. Without the amortization of the premium it appears that the interest expense was $1,000 the first year ($6,000 interest less $5,000 premium) and $6,000 the remaining four years for a total of $25,000. Each year should bear the same expense as any other and this is accomplished by the premium amortization. The corporation received $105,-000 for the bonds. At maturity the corporation will pay the face value $100,000 and during the five-year life of the bonds it will pay $30,000 in interest. The total cost of the bonds is $130,000 (amount paid out) less $105,-000 (amount received) which is $25,000. This amount should be divided among the years of life of the bonds equally.

If bonds, face value $100,000, 4 percent, are sold for $95,000, the entry would be:

Cash	$95,000	
Discount on Bonds Payable	5,000	
Bonds Payable		$100,000

Discount on bonds is classified as a deferred charge because it will add to the charge for interest as it is amortized. The payment of the interest is recorded as follows:

Bond Interest Cost	$4,000	
Cash		$4,000

Assuming the life of the bonds to be five years as before, the entry to amortize the discount would be:

Bond Interest Cost	$1,000	
Discount on Bonds Payable		$1,000

The payment of $4,000 interest and the amortization of the discount, $1,000, makes the total cost of the bonds for each year $5,000 and the total cost of the five years' life of the bonds $25,000. The corporation's total cost of the bonds, $100,000 face plus $20,000 interest minus the cash received for the bonds, $95,000, is $25,000. This $25,000 should be divided equally among the five years of life. This is done when $1,000 of the discount are added to the $4,000 interest expense each year for a cost of $5,000 each year for five years.

In the illustrations used it was assumed that the bonds were sold at the beginning of a fiscal year for the sake of simplicity. If ten $1,000, 6 percent bonds, dated January 1, to mature in ten years, were sold two months later on March 1, the amortization fraction to be used on December 31 would be 10/118. If the bonds had been sold on January 1, the amortization fraction would have been 12/120 or 1/10. Since they were sold two months later it means that the total life of the bonds will be 118 months. Ten months of the life would be amortized the first year and twelve months the last nine years for a total of 118 months. If the bonds had been sold for $10,472 and the accrued interest on March 1, the entry would be as follows:

Cash	$10,572	
Bonds Payable		$10,000
Premium on Bonds Payable		472
Bond Interest Cost		100

No matter how many times during the year the interest is paid on the bonds, the amortization of the premium should be recorded at the end of the fiscal year, which is December 31 in this illustration. The entry to pay one year's interest on December 31 is as follows:

| Bond Interest Cost | $600 | |
| Cash | | $600 |

The entry to amortize 10/118 of the premium is as follows:

| Premium on Bonds Payable | $40 | |
| Bond Interest Cost | | $40 |

When posted, the bond interest cost account appears as follows:

Bond Interest Cost	
Dec. 31 payment $600	$100 (Accrued interest on March 1)
	40
Balance $460	

If bonds are retired at the end of any particular year of the bond's life, it is relatively simple to record. If one of the bonds in the previous example were retired at the end of the first year, the only additional entry needed would be to debit Bonds Payable and to credit Cash. If the bonds are retired *during* the fiscal year, the amortization of the premium or discount up to the time of the retirement must be recorded in order to obtain the profit or loss on the retirement of the bonds. Assume a sale of ten $1,000, 6 percent, ten-year bonds for $10,708 and the accrued interest on March 1. The bonds are dated January 1, and the interest is payable on Jan-

uary 1 and on July 1. The entry to record the sale of
the bonds:

Cash	$10,808	
Bonds Payable		$10,000
Premium on Bonds Payable		708
Bond Interest Cost		100

The entry to record the payment of interest on July 1:

Bond Interest Cost	$300	
Cash		$300

The entry to accrue interest on December 31:

Bond Interest Cost	$300	
Interest Payable		$300

The entry to amortize premium on December 31:

Premium on Bonds Payable	$60	
Bond Interest Cost		$60
(10/118 x $708)		

The entry to close Bond Interest Cost:

Profit and Loss Summary	$440	
Bond Interest Cost		$440

The entry to reverse the adjusting entry:

Interest Payable	$300	
Bond Interest Cost		$300

The entry to record the payment of interest January 1:

Bond Interest Cost	$300	
Cash		$300

The corporation retires one of the $1,000 bonds, or 1/10 of the total, on April 1 following for $1,100 and the accrued interest. All of the entries over the life of the bonds have been recorded step by step, so no doubt could remain in anyone's mind as to what had taken place. At this point the book value of the bonds represented by the accounts is the book value on January 1, three months before. The book value on April 1 must now be determined. The easiest way to determine this is to amortize the premium for three more months. The entry to amortize 3/118 of the premium:

Premium on Bonds Payable	$18	
Bond Interest Cost		$18

This entry gives the correct book value of the bonds on April 1. The balance of the premium is $630 and the balance of the bonds payable is $10,000. If the corporation retires 1/10 of the book value ($10,630) for $1,100, the loss on the retirement will be $37. The entry:

Bonds Payable	$1,000	
Premium on Bonds Payable	63	
Bond Interest Cost	15	
Loss on Retirement of Bonds	37	
Cash		$1,115

The interest charge of $15 is the interest for three months on the $1,000 bond that is being retired. The entry to record the payment of interest on the next July 1:

Bond Interest Cost	$270	
Cash		$270
(Interest on $9,000 for six months)		

The entry to accrue interest on December 31:

Bond Interest Cost	$270	
Interest Payable		$270

The entry to amortize premium on December 31:

Premium on Bonds Payable	$48.60	
Bond Interest Cost		$48.60
(9/118 x (9/10 x $708)		

On April 1 the entire premium was amortized for three months. At that time the corporation retired 1/10 of the bonds. The corporation had 9/10 of the bonds outstanding for the entire year, so 9/10 of the original premium should be amortized on December 31. Another way to record would be to amortize 3/118 of 1/10 of the premium on April 1, then amortize 12/118 of 9/10 of the premium on December 31. The first method seems easier to record because when the book value of the entire bond issue is determined on April 1, it is easy to determine the book value of the fraction to be retired. If the amortization is up to date on April 1, it is only necessary to record amortization from that time until the end of the year. There is no real understanding of accounting for a bond issue until one can record an issue sold between interest dates, the retirement of a portion of the issue in a succeeding period, the payment of interest, and the amortization of the premium or discount for the entire life of the bonds.

When serial bonds have been issued, the amount of premium or discount to be amortized must be determined by the bonds outstanding method. Since serial bonds are redeemed regularly, the amount of the amortization should decrease as the amount of the bonds outstanding decrease. Assume a sale of $100,000 of serial bonds on January 1, 1970, $20,000 of which are to be redeemed each succeeding January 1 for five years. These 6 percent bonds are sold for $105,000. In order to determine the proper amortization amounts a bond outstanding table should be prepared.

1970	$100,000	10/30 x $5,000 =	$1,666.67
1971	80,000	8/30 x 5,000 =	1,333.33
1972	60,000	6/30 x 5,000 =	1,000.00
1973	40,000	4/30 x 5,000 =	666.67
1974	20,000	2/30 x 5,000 =	333.33
	$300,000		$5,000.00

As can be seen from the table the amount of the premium to be amortized each year becomes less as the bonds outstanding decrease. This method is similar to the reducing fraction method of determining depreciation charges.

Chapter XXXIII

ADMIXTIO

FOR THOSE WHO SEEM to be adept or have developed a desire to continue the study of accounting, a preview of the general accounting courses and specialized areas of study are presented.

Accounting Principles

Accounting principles offers a more concentrated study of Sole Proprietorships, Partnerships and Corporations. Detail work is involved and usually time is given to practice sets. Attention is paid to accounting techniques. Some specialized areas of accounting, such as manufacturing, can be introduced depending on the length of the course and the wishes of the instructor.

A course in accounting principles is usually one year in length.

Intermediate Accounting

Intermediate accounting is difficult to classify. In most textbooks, the course begins with a review of accounting principles. The tables of contents of intermediate accounting textbooks are very similar to the tables of contents of accounting principles textbooks. However, intermediate accounting goes deeper into each of the subjects presented and some new areas of accounting are introduced, notably the preparation of comparative statements, the analysis of financial statements, and the statement of application of funds. Intermediate accounting adds much to one's understanding of estimating inventories by the introduction of additional methods other than the gross profits method which is ordinarily taught in the accounting principles course. These additional methods include the relative sales value, the retail inventory, estimating inventories in manufacturing, and estimating profits in construction on a degree of completion basis.

Intermediate accounting varies in length from one quarter to one year.

Comparative Statements

In the preparation of comparative statements two or more statements such as profit and loss or balance sheets are placed on the same report for better comparison. Reports of the current year become more meaningful when compared with one or more previous years.

Statement Analysis

Statement analysis is a study of various ratios and measurements based on the data of a single fiscal period, such as the ratio of owner's capital to the liabilities, or the ratio of plant and equipment to long-term debt, the ratio of sales to assets, and the book value per shares of stock.

Funds Statement

The statement of application of funds is an attempt to picture the flow of working capital through a business in a fiscal period. It attempts to determine the total purchasing power that was provided for a business and exactly to what this purchasing power was applied. It goes beyond the preparation of "cash flow" reports or where the cash came from and where it went. For instance, if a machine was purchased at a cost of $10,000, with a down payment of $1,000 and a promissory note given for the remainder, $1,000 of purchasing power was provided by the decrease of the asset Cash, $9,000 of purchasing power was provided by the increase of the liability Notes Payable, and the $10,000 in purchasing power was applied to the increase of the asset Machinery. Only $1,000 in cash changed hands, but $10,000 in purchasing power was provided and $10,000 in purchasing power was applied. The statement of application of funds is becoming increasingly important in presenting the financial condition of a business and the demand for a statement of this kind is sure to become greater as stockholders and management learn of better ways to present a picture of the operations of a business. The statement has other names such as "funds statement," "financial benefits employed," and even such names as "where got and where gone."

Methods of Estimating Inventories

Gross Profits

In estimating inventories by the gross profits method the goods available for sale are determined as if a profit and loss statement were being prepared. Instead of subtracting the ending merchandise inventory from the goods available for sale to get the cost of goods sold, as is usually the case, the process is reversed. The cost of goods sold is subtracted from the goods available to get the ending inventory when someone wishes to estimate the inventory in case of fire or in the preparation of monthly statements. If a firm has a consistent mark-up or an average mark-up of 20 percent of sales, the cost of goods sold can easily be determined by multiplying the net sales by 20 percent. If 20 percent is added to cost to determine sales price the sales must be divided by 1.20 to determine the cost of sales.

Relative Sales Value

The relative sales value method of estimating inventories is almost the only logical way to determine the inventory value of building lots when a parcel of land is purchased and then subdivided. If $20,000 was paid for a parcel of land and the land was divided into lots, some lots would be on high ground, some would have trees, some would be large and some would be small. At least they would probably have different selling prices. To simplify the illustration, assume that the parcel was divided into twenty lots, ten of which were priced to sell at $1,000 each and ten priced at $2,000 each. One of the $2,000 lots was sold. What is the profit? Using the relative sales value method, the cost is determined as follows:

$$10 \times \$\,1,000 = \$10,000$$
$$10 \times 2,000 = \underline{20,000}$$
$$30,000$$

$$\frac{10,000}{30,000} \times \$20,000 = \$\,6,666.67 \text{ (price of 10 lots)}$$

$$\frac{20,000}{30,000} \times 20,000 = 13,333.33 \text{ (price of 10 lots)}$$

One of the lots priced to sell at $2,000 would result in a profit of $666.67 when sold. One of the lots priced to sell at $1,000 would result in a profit of $333.33 when sold.

Retail Inventory

The retail inventory method of estimating inventories uses the principle of determining the goods available for sale at cost and retail, and obtaining the gross profit percentage by arithmetic. The net sales are subtracted from the goods available for sale at retail which leaves the ending inventory at retail. This is reduced to cost by arithmetic.

Manufacturing

Any manufactured item from a safety pin to an atomic submarine has only three elements of cost, the cost of the materials used, the cost of the labor employed, and the cost of the overhead or burden. The reason there can be only three elements of cost in a manufactured product is that all other manufacturing expenses not included in the prime costs of materials and direct labor are called overhead costs.

In one system of manufacturing accounting two extra columns are inserted on the work sheet and all the manufacturing costs are placed in these columns. The difference between the two columns is the cost of goods manufactured, and this amount is placed in the cost column of the profit and loss section of the work sheet.

The ending inventory of finished goods is adjusted in the same manner as merchandise inventory, i.e., credit the old inventory, debit the new, and do the reverse to the profit and loss summary account. The ending inventory of raw materials is adjusted in much the same way except the opposite debits and credits are made to a manufacturing summary account. The goods in process account is adjusted in the same manner as the raw materials account. In the cost of goods manufactured columns of a work sheet will be found all of the manufacturing expenses such as depreciation of machinery, indirect labor and all expenses identified with manufacturing, together with the manufacturing summary account which contains the beginning and ending inventories of raw materials and goods in process because of the entries which adjusted these accounts.

Estimating Profits in Construction

Determining profits on construction by using a degree of completion basis can lower taxes by keeping the contractor in a lower tax bracket. If a contractor bids $100,000 on a construction job that he estimates will cost $80,000 he figures to make $20,000 on the job when it is complete. If his fiscal period ends before the construction is completed, he is allowed by Internal Revenue to take up profits by the use of a formula. If he spends $20,000 before the fiscal period ends he may determine his profit in this manner:

$$\frac{\text{Costs of construction } \$20,000}{\text{Total estimated costs } 80,000} \quad x \quad \begin{array}{l}\text{Estimated profit} \\ \$20,000\end{array} = \$5,000$$

Cost Accounting

There are so many cost accounting systems and miscellaneous cost factors, such as accounting for distribution or accounting for by-products, that a separate course in cost accounting is justified, and in some instances a course in advanced cost accounting should be elected.

Process Cost Accounting

Process cost accounting is a system of accounting that attempts to determine the cost of an entire process such as the manufacture of paint. The total cost of the process is divided by the number of gallons to get the cost per gallon.

Job Order Cost Accounting

Job order cost accounting is an attempt to determine the costs of certain jobs as they are ordered for customers or for the warehouse. In this system an account, Goods in Process, is charged with the three elements of cost, Raw Materials, Direct Labor, and Overhead. When jobs are completed, Goods in Process is credited and Finished Goods is debited. When sales are made, Cost of Sales is debited for the cost price and Finished Goods is credited; the retail price is recorded in the usual way to Accounts Receivable and Sales. This system makes much use of perpetual inventories and subsidiary ledgers.

Standard Cost Accounting

Standard cost accounting is a system of determining in advance of production the costs of the materials, labor and manufacturing expenses (overhead or burden) as near as it can be determined by the best brains of a management team. This cannot be done of course, but the Standard costs can be recorded and the variations from standard can be determined to help explain why costs are more or less than predicted.

The various systems of cost accounting may be offered in one course of cost accounting or they may be offered independently as separate courses.

Advanced Accounting

Advanced accounting in nearly all instances brings opportunities for new experiences in new areas of accounting. This course is usually one year in length. Topics that have not been touched upon before, with the exception of a beginning review, are presented. These topics include joint ventures, consignments, installments, agencies, branches, consolidated statements, insolvencies, receiverships, estates and trusts. Some of these topics are included in Intermediate Accounting by some publishers of textbooks. A unit in actuarial science consisting of present and future values is usually taught in the advanced accounting course. Actuarial science is also taught in mathematics courses.

Municipal and Governmental Accounting

Municipal and governmental accounting is taught as a separate course in some colleges and is included in the advanced accounting course in others. Municipal and governmental accounting is concerned with general and special funds, the principles and procedures applicable to state and local governments, school districts, and institutions such as hospitals and colleges. Anyone who contemplates employment with state, local or federal government agencies should certainly include a course of this type in his accounting preparation.

Income Tax Accounting

Internal Revenue decrees, the Internal Revenue Code of 1954, and the effect of federal income taxes on accounting procedures afford a source of study at all levels of accounting. Anyone who is seriously considering accounting as a profession should take special courses in federal income taxes when the opportunity arises. Those who are not contemplating careers in accounting can obtain valuable knowledge for personal use by enrolling in these courses. One can become quite expert in the technique of filling out income tax blanks and in the interpretation of Internal Revenue laws without becoming an expert accountant.

Accounting Systems

A course in accounting systems usually emphasizes cost control, the principles underlying the establishment of complete accounting systems and the application of such principles to typical business organizations. Anyone preparing for a career in accounting should take a course in accounting systems if possible.

Data Processing

The impact of data processing on the accounting profession is already enormous and will continue to increase in the future. Courses in data processing are in the formative stages. Prospective accountants should take courses of this type in order to learn the relationship of machine accounting to generally accepted accounting principles. This area offers exciting new careers for college graduates with an accounting background.

C.P.A. Problems

In intermediate accounting, advanced accounting, and in other upper division courses in accounting one finds many problems labeled A.I.C.P.A.- or A.I.C.P.A.-adapted. This means that the problem was prepared by the American Institute of Certified Public Accountants and that the problem or one similar to it has been given on a certified public accountant's examination. Many colleges use these problems and others as material for an intensive course as preparation for the examination.

Auditing

To anyone who has become knowledgeable in accounting, auditing is probably the most interesting of all the courses they have an opportunity to take. Correcting other accountants errors, dealing with the various quirks and machinations of human nature, and certifying to the correctness of accounting statements are fascinating. The prospective auditor learns that he must be liberal in his thinking and tolerant of the techniques of others. In auditing a set of records that have no cash account in the ledger, he may discover that the book-keeper can convince him that it is a waste of time to keep an accurate check-stub record and also a cash account. He may find that instead of making closing entries and posting a firm merely removes the nominal accounts from the ledger and cannot be convinced that there is a better way.

Most college and university graduates with a major in accounting or a major in business administration with a strong emphasis on accounting obtain employment as auditors. This is a natural consequence, since in all probability it seems more interesting to be able to work with other people and with other people's figures and mistakes than with one's own.

Many other specialized courses in accounting are available in some institutions. One may take hospital accounting, agricultural accounting, social security accounting, accounting for high school principals, and many others. No one should neglect his general education. After all, promotion into management and progress up the management ladder will depend more on how a person has developed his ability to reason, to make sound judgments, to get along with people and to lead and inspire others, as well as on his desire to continue his education than on the numerous techniques he has acquired.

Index

167

Other SIGNET and MENTOR Titles of Interest